This book is dedicated to my mother, Kathryn Morris.

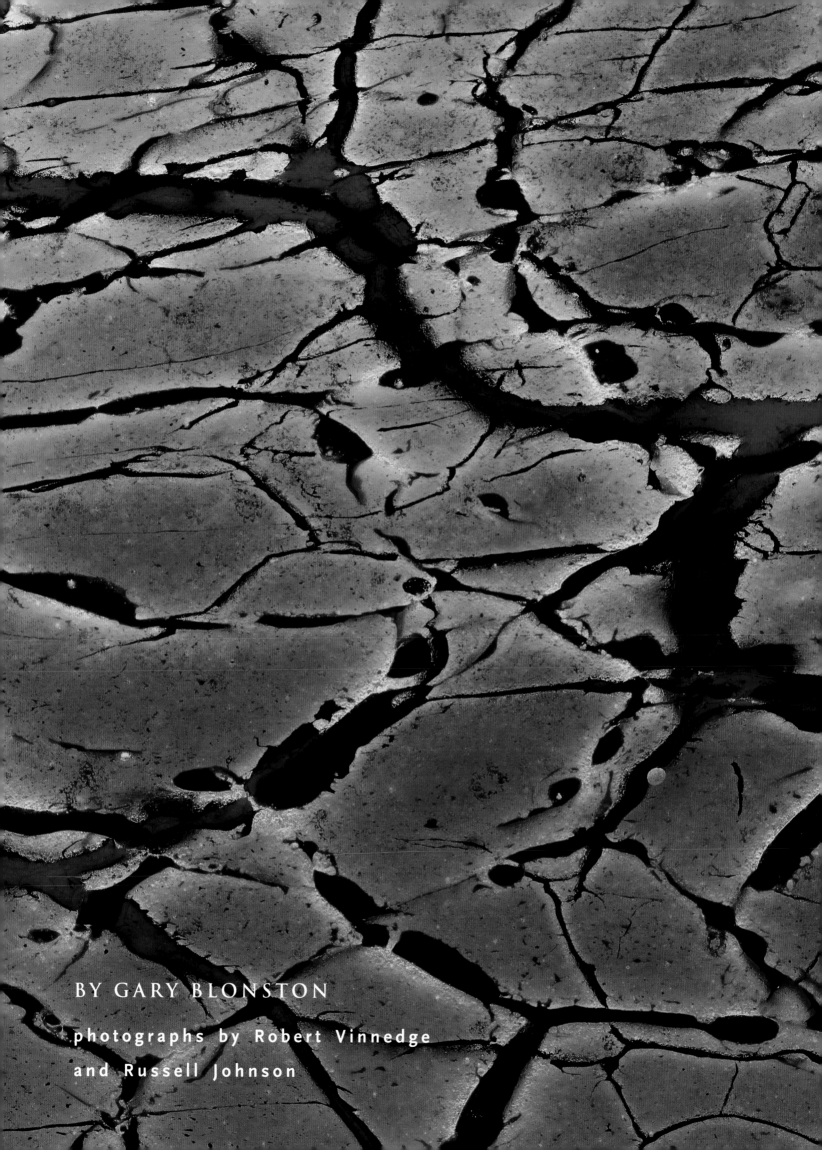

BY GARY BLONSTON

photographs by Robert Vinnedge
and Russell Johnson

# WILLIAM
# MORRIS

## artifacts / glass

ABBEVILLE PRESS PUBLISHERS
NEW YORK · LONDON · PARIS

Copyright © 1996 by William Morris
Text copyright © 1996 by Gary Blonston
Photographs © 1996 by Robert Vinnedge, except
pages 108–27 by Russell Johnson

All rights reserved under international copyright
conventions. No part of this book may be repro-
duced or utilized in any form or by any means,
electronic or mechanical, including photocopy-
ing, recording, or by any information storage and
retrieval system, without permission in writing
from the publisher. Inquiries should be addressed
to Abbeville Publishing Group, 488 Madison
Avenue, New York, NY 10022. The text of this
book was set in Scala Sans with display type set
in Trajan. Printed and bound in Singapore by
CS Graphics.

First Edition
10 9 8 7 6 5 4 3 2 1

Library of Congress Cataloging-in-
Publication Data
Blonston, Gary.
    William Morris : artifacts—glass / Gary
Blonston ; photographs by Robert Vinnedge
and Russell Johnson.
        p.   cm.
    Includes bibliographical references.
    ISBN 0-7892-0167-4
    1. Morris, William—Criticism and interpre-
tation. 2. Morris, William—Catalogs. I. Title.
    NK5198.M585858 1996          95-41449
    730'.92—dc20

Edited by Holle Simmons
Designed by Brian Ellis Martin and John D. Berry
Produced by Marquand Books, Inc.

Front cover: *Artifact: Pouch,* 1995. 18 x 18 x 15 in.
Private collection (AP595.02.05).
Back cover inset: *Suspended Artifact: Antlered
Spoon with Tusks,* 1995. 29 x 20 x 9 in. Collection
of the artist (SA395.04.07).
Page 1: *Suspended Artifact: Lashed Tusks with
Legged Pouch,* 1995. 21 x 21 x 5 in. Private
collection (SA395.14.06).
Page 5: *Artifacts: Tusks,* 1992. 12 x 24 x 18 in.
Collection of Alan Benaroya (AT392.19.08).
Page 6: Detail, *Suspended Artifact: Baleen and
Walrus Tusk,* 1995 (see p. 97).

The quotation by Matthew Kangas, appearing on
page 28, has been excerpted from *Glass Maga-
zine,* no. 55 (spring 1994) and is used by permission of the publisher.

NATIONAL
ENDOWMENT
FOR THE
ARTS

The artwork featured in this book was funded in
part by a grant from the National Endowment for
the Arts.

# CONTENTS

# FOREWORD

Many things go into the realization of a great artist like William Morris. First, of course, there is an innate talent which can be tapped and expressed as with no ordinary person. Then there is the artist's dedication to his or her chosen medium and the motivation to honor the progress toward its mastery. Finally, there is the presence of a stimulating environment in which to continually develop the creative spirit.

Such a fertile environment was created when the "Studio Glass Movement" began in 1962 with the famous Toledo workshops led by Harvey Littleton and Dominick Labino. Littleton, a professor of ceramics, and Labino, a glass chemist and engineer, developed a small furnace that could melt glass at relatively low temperatures. This innovation allowed glass artists to make their work in a studio setting rather than in a factory, thereby creating a revolution in the field of glass. Soon, courses in glassmaking were offered at universities across the country, and in 1971 the renowned Pilchuck Glass School was founded in the Pacific Northwest by Dale Chihuly, one of Littleton's first students.

It was amid this highly charged atmosphere that William Morris came to Pilchuck as a staff member and later became one of Chihuly's most valued assistants. In the span of twenty years Morris's genius for blowing glass allowed him to transcend the technical challenges of the medium to create works of art that are sought after by museums and collectors worldwide.

Morris's Suspended Artifacts and Canopic Jars produce a magical connection in viewers' minds between today's reality and the prehistoric past. The works are relevant and contemporary yet provocatively ancient. Are these tusks, bones, and shards newly unearthed artifacts or are they gathers blown and formed in the sophisticated studios of contemporary glass artists? Like the waxen death masks of ancient Greece and the memento mori in *vanitas* paintings, the viewer is drawn in by a sense of redoubtable otherworldliness and must make his or her personal connection between life and death and the art being confronted.

I often stood in the gallery at the Metropolitan Museum of Art while Morris's *Suspended Artifact* was on display. Inevitably, visitors on their way from the galleries of African, American, and Oceanic art to the twentieth-century art wing would stop, captivated by the provocative and forceful yet unfamiliar work. As it became clear that the art was contemporary blown glass, the viewer would be further drawn in by its virtuosity. The experience was intensely personal, and the moment of revelation exultant.

In a 1957 speech Marcel Duchamp said, "Millions of artists create, only a few thousand are discussed or accepted by the spectator and many less again are consecrated by posterity."

William Morris will surely be among the consecrated.

**Jane Adlin**
**Department of Twentieth Century Art**
**Metropolitan Museum of Art, New York**

# WILLIAM

WILLIAM MORRIS CREATES some of the most unusual and compelling objects ever to emerge from a glass-blower's pipe, but it is not in his nature to offer elaborate esthetic musings to explain himself. No arcane artspeak rationalizes all those tusks and spear-heads, skins and bones. His intention, he says, is simple, specific, and direct—to prod that remnant part of humanity's brain that still senses the ageless inter-twinings of life and death, still knows the adrenal jolt of living in a world shared with wild things, still tingles with the certainty that primal mystery crouches just beyond the light of ancient fires. Here is the death mask of a wolf, suspended beside an etched quiver of primitive weapons. Here is a skull, a great tooth, a burial urn, a pendulous gourd, a pile of bones arranged in a makeshift boat. What do these things mean, where did they come from?

Morris answers in shrugs. He only raises the questions, he says. The an-swers lie in the eye, in the imagina-tion and in the deep, almost archetypal memory of the beholder. He has been listening to people piece together an-swers for more than fifteen years now, as growing numbers of Morris admir-ers, half-repelled, half-seduced, have confronted his archaeological visions and conjured their own imaginings of

harsh prehistory and the power of na-ture. "There's sort of a common thread people have when they encounter primi-tive objects. The impressions people get tend to be the same," he says. "The story lines differ, but the themes are the same. . . . No matter how far from these objects we get, there's a natural fascina-tion about them. We really can't leave who we are."

Morris's work is all in glass, astonish-ment enough; visitors come to his stu-dio from around the globe to see how these amazing shapes and deceptive surfaces come to be. But what has put his art in the galleries and museums of the world is more than just an artisan's expertise. The things he makes, these "found objects" of natural man and beast, bridge the millennia.

Look: a fragment of ancient pottery, an antler, an arrowhead, a faint graven image on flat stone. The experience is as old as childhood—that moment in the forest, or on a rocky hillside, or at the edge of a stream, when something odd and stirring suddenly seems to jump out of time and present itself, here and now. Ask any archaeologist, any anthropolo-gist, anyone who ever found an aban-doned bird's nest or the print of a shell in limestone. They know the feeling.

**Suspended Artifact: Walrus Tusk with Wolf Mask and Antler, 1995**

In his glassblowing studio, Morris holds high a long, primitive spoon, just finished, still fixed to his blowpipe and glowing orange-hot. Its dark, textured handle seems to be an antelope horn, and that horn seems lashed by a heavy thong to a dark-veined bowl of stone or bone or palmate antler. It is a stunning piece that reminds Morris of the traditional horn spoons made by Indians in the Pacific Northwest. He gives it his ultimate seal of approval: "Wouldn't you love to *find* something like this?"

Upon reflection, he says something else, more to the point: "It isn't the finding; it's the imagining."

William Morris grew up roaming the hills above Carmel, California, imagining the Indians who roamed there before him. He dug pot shards from burial mounds almost in his backyard. He found arrowheads in the caves. In the wildlands, he found a place to be. "I was very comfortable in the woods at fourteen," Morris says, "out several nights at a time."

Some years later, he remembers wandering above timberline in the high Sierra, in an area flaked with obsidian, when "right on the surface, there was this beautiful flint point." It was hundreds of years old, dating to a time when traders carried the hard stone of the mountains to willing bargainers by the sea.

Morris remembers the moment he came upon the arrow tip as if he had walked that historic trail only this morning. From those moments of discovery, from that sensitivity to the evidence of early human societies, rose the art he makes today.

Morris's life as an artist was not an automatic, fated certainty, though. He took ceramics classes in high school and art studies in college, but he was more than a little reckless, and in fact, in his young life Morris tried a little of everything. At twenty, he was drifting, driving a truck for a place north of Seattle called Pilchuck Glass School.

Pilchuck is the brainchild of Dale Chihuly, a remarkable pioneer in American glass art. In the mid-1970s, just as his reputation as a glass artist was taking off, he lost an eye in an auto accident, and his lack of depth perception prevented him from ever blowing glass again without a team of technicians to do the hands-on work. Still, by the time Morris met him at Pilchuck, Chihuly's creative genius and marketing savvy already were transforming the Seattle area into a unique center of contemporary glass art—and transforming glass into a whole new category of American artistic expression.

Morris became Chihuly's protégé and ultimately his gaffer and chief glassblower. Strong and capable, he helped Chihuly produce some of the most eye-filling, colorful—and huge—abstract glass creations the art world had ever seen. In return, Chihuly became Morris's mentor and guide, and the two still maintain a close friendship. But it was inevitable that someone with Morris's talents as a glassblower would set out to find his own creative heart. What was less predictable was that this onetime studio gaffer who made his reputation blowing Chihuly's kaleidoscopic, fluid shapes would become internationally recognized for creating a somber, earth-toned retelling of the archaeological past.

**Detail,**
**Suspended Artifact,**
**1991**

Tentative at first, he started where most glass artists do—making decorated vessels, testing the possibilities of color and contour. But soon Morris's shapes began changing from mostly decorative to sober and contemplative, the colors from brilliant to subdued, the surfaces from glint to shadow, the ideas steadily moving closer to the ground and deeper in time. Gradually he stopped making containers for their own sake and started making things they might carry—bones and arrows, and animal heads surmounting stylized vessels, reminiscent of ancient Egyptian funerary urns. He tried out techniques for shaping the long polished tusks of fantasy pachyderms and the twisting unicorn spear of the narwhal. His skeletal assemblages, tangles of bone and tusk up to thirty-six feet long, were so stark and intriguing that one such installation became part of the permanent glass collection in a downtown Seattle commercial center, another the centerpiece of a busy passenger area at Seattle's airport, capable of stopping the busiest travelers in their tracks. Some viewers complained that these things must have been taken illegally. A sign went up: It's glass. Morris was recapturing his childhood thrall, and so were the people who saw his work.

Morris had his first major solo exhibition in Seattle in 1980, when he was twenty-three. His career and his popularity have grown steadily ever since. Today, his art can be found in such important collections as Paris's Musée des Arts Décoratifs, London's Victoria and Albert Museum, New York's Metropolitan Museum of Art, the Los Angeles County Museum of Art, and the Hokkaidō Museum of Modern Art in Japan. Corporate collectors have mounted his work in such prestigious environs as Rockefeller Center in New York, the IBM Corporation's facility in Tulsa, Oklahoma, and the Microsoft Corporation headquarters in Redmond, Washington. And Morris is represented in major private collections around the world.

The artist behind these increasingly celebrated and formidable works is formidable himself: tall, athletic, and boyish, with longish black hair that he slicks back into a short ponytail when he works. In his studio, in sandals, sleeveless tee shirts, and glasses tinted against the gas-fired glare, Morris embodies the style and mien of the West Coast. But his is the ethic of the non-urban West, wary of pretense, jealous of space. He drives a pick-up truck, rides a motorcycle, lives in a log house that looks to the mountains northeast of Seattle, hunts deer and elk with a bow. He works four days a week, and on those days gets up with the sun and often retires when it does, too. He tends to avoid big cities and big groups and news and politics and neckties, drinks non-alcoholic beer, eats game meat, and when the mood strikes, will take off on his motorcycle or an airplane bound for out-of-the-way places. He is smart and articulate and laughs easily, but he probably would prefer not seeing some of this in print, because normally Morris doesn't give a lot of himself away, even when talking about his art, which he calls simply "the work."

He goes at it as if it were just that—work, on schedule, day after day, his small crew dependably in place in the early morning, toiling hard and steadily in front of the ovens' blazing heat with only a 9 A.M. stop for a breakfast they call lunch. If he didn't do it that way, he says, he would never get anything done.

He tries not to think through his artistic ideas in detail; he's too often disappointed at the result. "If I'm dealing with it at the conscious level," he says, "then it only comes from what I know, and if it's only what I know, I'm not getting anywhere. . . . That stuff that comes from your gut—you can't pull it up whenever you want. . . . So I allow myself to become the victim of mood and circumstance. It might be hit or miss, but you hit a lot more."

And so he takes his chances, as the best glassblowers often do, seeing what will evolve at the end of the pipe, in the heat, at the whim of gravity's pull and an artist's eye. And when it's over, he claims he has no better explanation or interpretation than anyone else for what he has just created.

It is almost as though Morris is still out on the trail, still a bit adrift, waiting to see what will happen and what he will find, as delighted as anyone else that, so often, it turns out right.

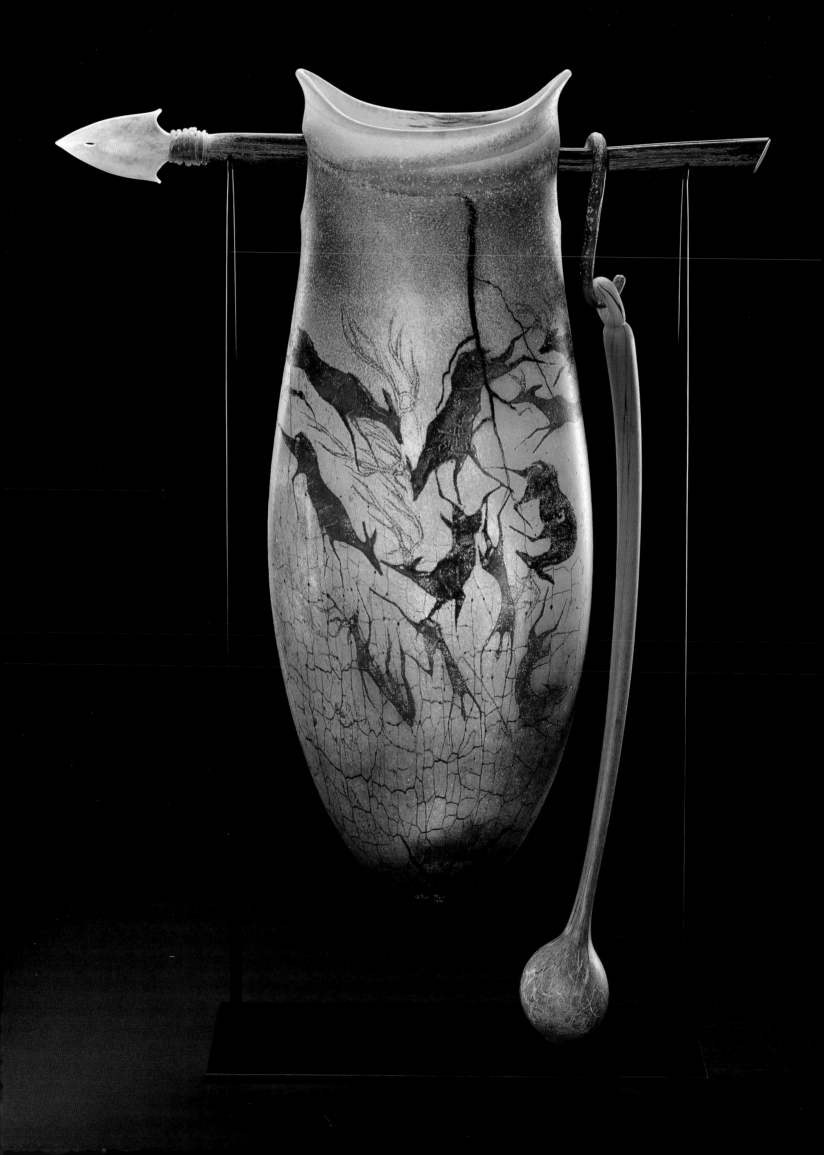

# ART

Throughout his career as a studio glass artist, William Morris seems to have pursued a fairly orderly course, a timeline of sorts, through the natural and archaeological past. But in fact, his glass is as much a record of what has happened to Morris himself, the evolution of his esthetic sense from cool to warm, and the expansion of his technical knowledge of the almost limitless possibilities for creating texture and shape in glass.

Over the years, the names he has given his various series offer a rough record of those changes—from the relatively straightforward, geologically inspired works of the 1980s, Standing Stone, Stone Vessel, River Rock, to the more anthropological and complex ideas of the 1990s, Burial Urn, Suspended Artifact, Canopic Jar.

It seems another artist altogether who made the early works—austere vessels, monoliths, and rock arrangements virtually unrelieved by signs of life. Slowly, though, Morris began decorating the faces of his vessel shapes with images of men and animals, and then abandoned his early stones and vessels altogether. Forms inspired by past and present living things began to command his attention. Yet even that phase of his work—early skeletal shapes, antlers, and tusks—produced only representations of life in memoriam, the cold remains.

**Suspended Artifact:**
**Urn with Orinka,**
**1994**

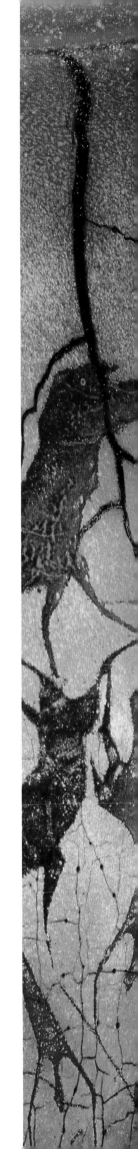

*Above and right:*
Burial Urn, 1991

Suspended Burial Urn,
1991

Detail, Garnering,
(narwhal tusks and
skulls), 1990

Artifact: Shard
with Bone Pins,
1993

In the 1990s, his art has moved farther, to a realm where prehistory still is his inspiration, but life, real life—ancient humanity's assertive presence—is evident in almost everything he does.

Where once Morris created boulders of glass or marked inscrutable lines and shapes on the swelled sides of glass containers, now he reinterprets marbled burial urns from Pharaonic Egypt and tops them with the heads of North American animals—antelope, deer, and hawks. So symmetrical and proportionate are these canopic jars that it is hard to believe they aren't the product of a potter's wheel rather than the freehand work of a glass sculptor.

Detail, Suspended
Artifact, 1995

Canopic Jar: Giant
Eland, 1995

Canopic Jar: Big Horn
Sheep, 1995

Where once he arranged skeletons in big, message-y juxtapositions of glossy black and white human bones, or even bigger monuments to encounters between animal and man, now he ties a single antler to a single tusk with a glass thong and leaves it to the viewer to wonder whether some ancient shaman might also have made such a thing, and why.

Where once he arranged natural shapes in huge, almost random scatterings, now he hangs side-by-side collections of small, human-scale objects inspired by the tools and weapons of early man, obviously selected and positioned because of their relationships of form, color, and meaning.

**Suspended Artifact: Pouch with Antler and Gourd, 1994**

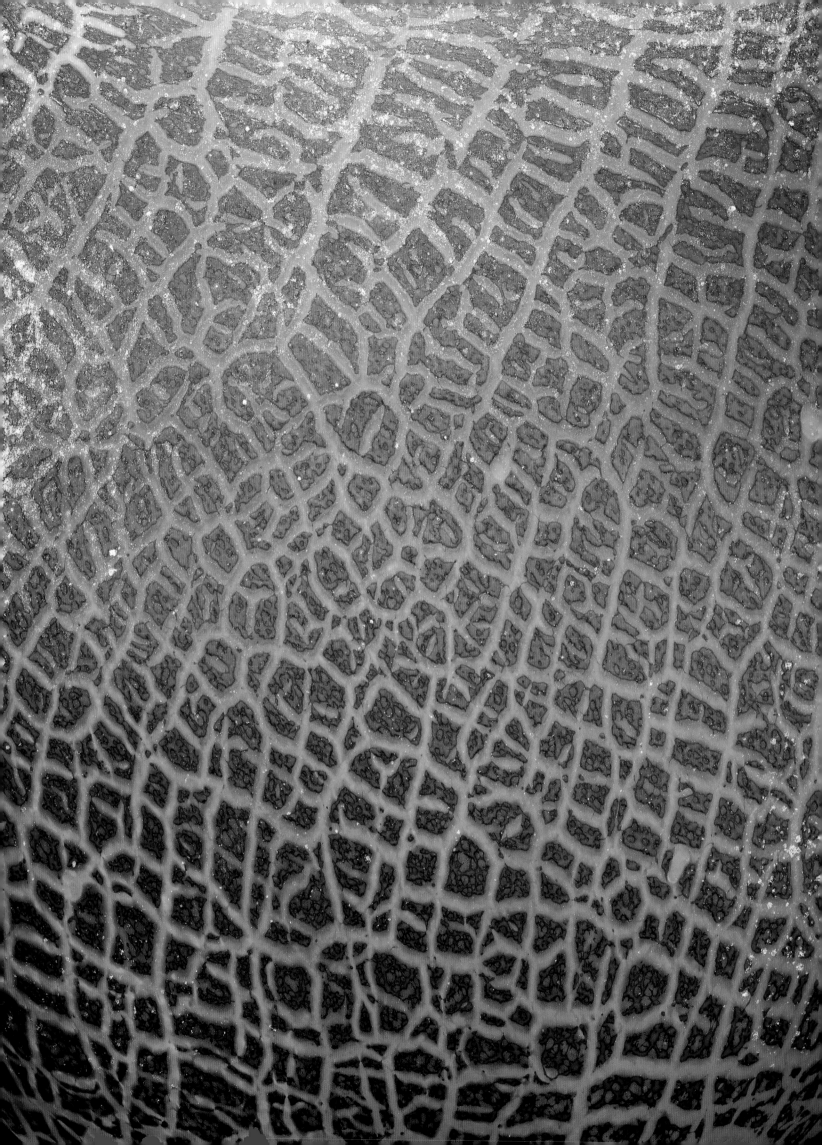

Detail, Suspended
Artifact, 1995

And where once he produced glass with
the gleam of transparency or the glint of
polished surfaces, now he seeks such
accuracy of shape and texture that the
outcome often belies the fact he is working in glass at all. Morris goes so far as
to say that, over the years, he has dis-
covered there is a lot about the inherent
nature of glass that he doesn't even like.
"I love the luminosity and the way it
works," he says, "but if it's shiny, it loses
that internal glow because the light is
all reflected from the surface. . . . It's a
distraction from what I'd like the work to
say. . . . If that were the only quality the
material had to offer, then I'd probably
stop working in glass." Instead, in recent
years, he has studiously removed the
glassiness from his art, in favor of opac-
ity, sober tones, and textural depth that
seem far more like antler or wood or
stone than anything as manufactured
as glass.

Detail, Suspended
Artifact, 1995

He sees this journey from the chilly and alien to the sensual and familiar as a technical learning curve as much as an artistic shift. Over the years, trial and error and the guidance of masters from the ancestral home of glass artistry in Venice have taught him increasingly more sophisticated and effective techniques of shaping and finishing glass, and that knowledge has armed him with an ever-growing sense of exploration.

For instance, when he began making animal heads, destined for the lids of his canopic jars, he says, "I first thought it would be amazing if I could just put single spike antlers on one of these heads. And then it was an antler with two points, and then eventually six or eight, but it happened one point at a time."

"If I had been asked then about what I'm doing now, I would have said it was impossible. With the surfaces, it's the same. What I do with the surfaces now is something I'd never have imagined three years ago."

Artifact: Tusk, 1993

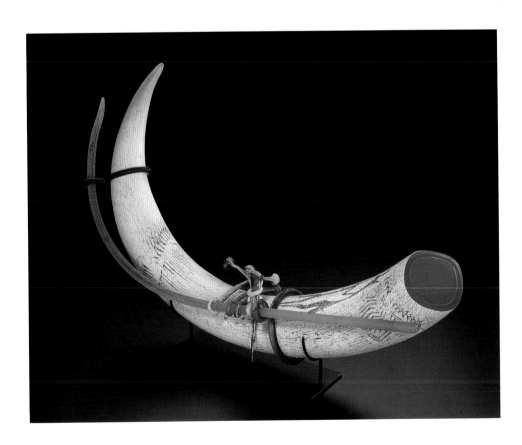

Canopic Jar: Fallow
Deer, 1994

Morris tends to talk about his work in technical terms, reluctant to offer meanings or metaphors. He leaves most of that to the art curators, critics, and historians, who are more than willing to plunge fervently into archeo-paleo-psycho-socio-cultural interpretations of his provocative images, at the same time arguing relentlessly about whether Morris's work is true art or mere craft.

An example from one curatorial enthusiast of Morris's work, Seattle-based Matthew Kangas:

> *Art-meaning resides in craft when it can invoke comparably poetic and metaphorical layers of meaning. Morris's work achieves this when critics are active interpreters, taking notice of his twin heritages of early abstract expressionism and West Coast clay sculpture. With its ties to earth and the birth of human societies, his art is socially engaged as well, affirming the need for community as well as coexistence with the animal world. Add to that the possibility that some of his art is chronicling a dying male culture of today: hunting.*

> *By reminding us of the ancient past, we are confronted in Morris's work by contrast with our troubled present. By avoiding the scolding character of political art, he proposes relief, an escape into the past that is really a window onto the present, a present that sidesteps systems and elevates custom, ritual and a masculinity under assault.*

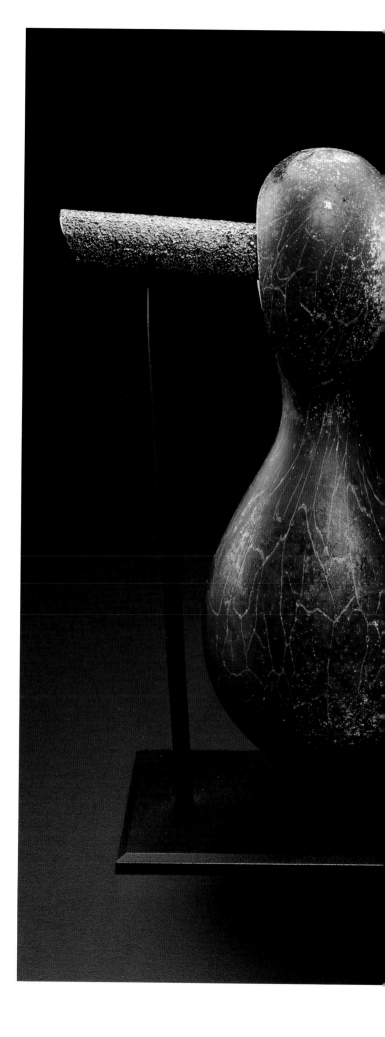

Suspended Artifact:
Burial Pouch with
Gourd, 1992

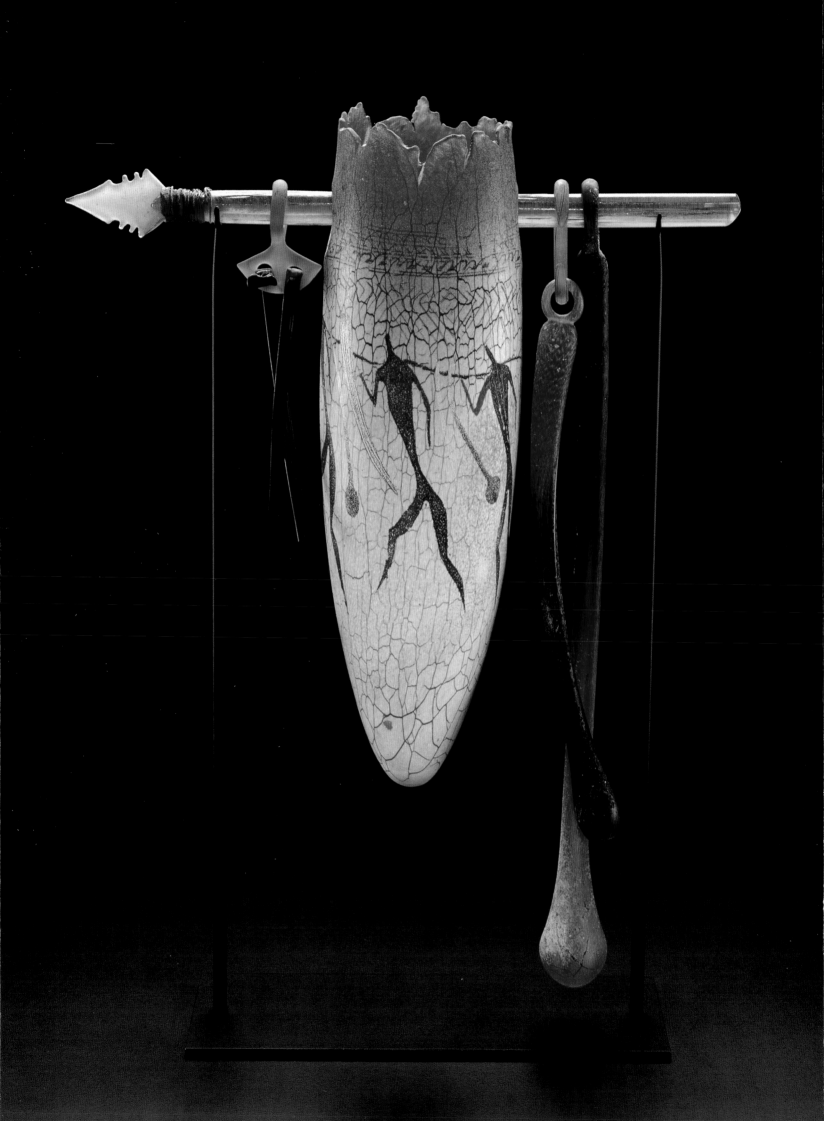

As for Morris, he says simply this: "I don't know why I am, or the audience is, so fascinated. But whatever it is, it isn't of a grandiose nature. It's much more subtle than that."

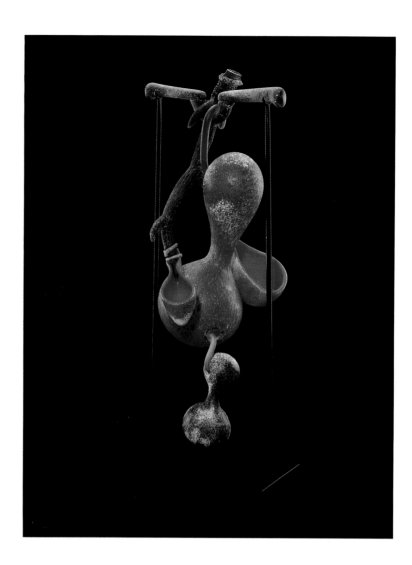

Suspended Artifact:
Antlered Spoon with
Gourds, 1994

Morris's inspirations in the 1990s, more than ever before, have been tools, weapons and ritual symbols, starting with a series of pieces he called Batons. The Batons are a bit puzzling, not quite explainable modifications of something like bones into something like clubs or ceremonial icons, long, primitive, and often translucent.

They are mounted upright on stands, related stylistically to a series of urns that he made to hang between vertical posts during the same period. The Petroglyphic Urns, like some of his earlier, more colorful and decorative vessels, bear compelling images that evoke ancient cave paintings and time-less stories of stalk, chase, and kill.

But both the Batons and the urns seem like ideas awaiting completion, isolated, stark, and disconnected, as if they were the beginnings of some larger notion yet to come. And in fact they were. Morris moved on quickly from these single objects and began experimenting with multiple forms that culminated in the collected "artifacts" that dominate his work to this day.

Suspended Artifact:
Orinkas, 1994

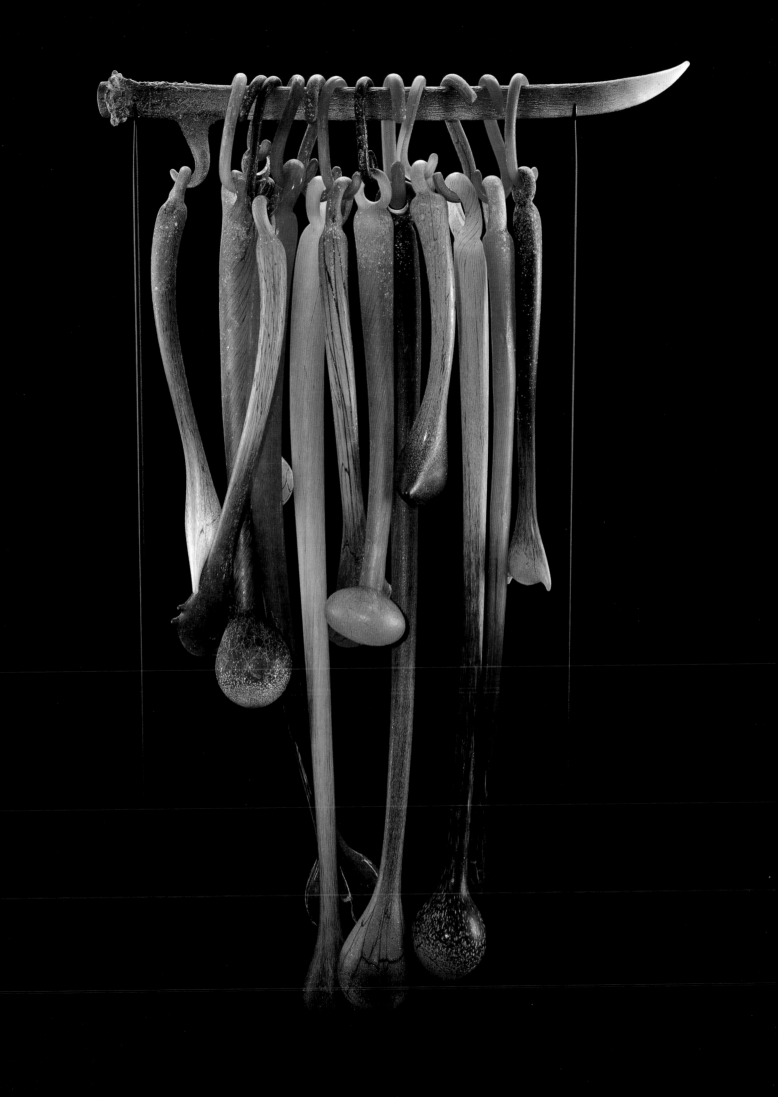

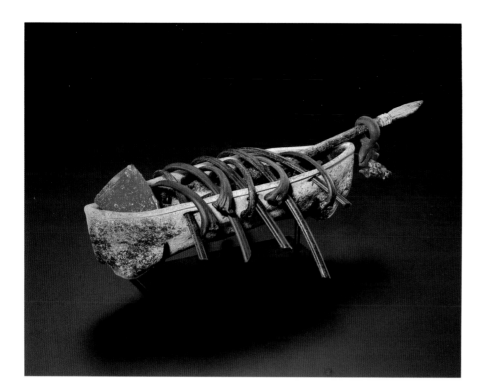

Burial Raft, 1993

One of the series that carried him from the urns to the artifact groups was a set of works called Burial Raft. Though much smaller than some of his huge, early arrangements of bones, they hearkened back to that time, in both form and message.

Typically in the raft series, a shallow canoe shape mounted on a two-poled stand is filled with an arrangement of bones and short lengths of spear presided over by a single skull. These clearly are not meant to represent the mere leftovers of some encounter in nature but to be part of a ritual, an otherworldly deliverance from here to . . . somewhere. The rafts were among his first pieces to suggest that some early human mind had a hand in the arrangement. At the same time, they were the last of Morris's works to display the literal objects of death and transformation, the end of an era that had established him as one of the important new glass artists of America. He made his last raft in 1993.

Burial Raft, 1991

Since then, his work has moved away from bones and skulls to focus almost exclusively on implements of the living, his intriguing collections of Suspended Artifacts.

"The biggest jump," he says, "was moving into artifacts." That shift of subject quite literally pulled the bottom out from under his art.

"They didn't have anything to stand on, and so they didn't hold together as single objects. The associations became more important. And then when they were suspended, there was no longer any randomness and happenstance. It became very deliberate."

The first attempts were with shapes he had at hand. "It took a while to work it out," Morris says, "but it was a whole new concept when I put something next to those urns, like a very simple tool."

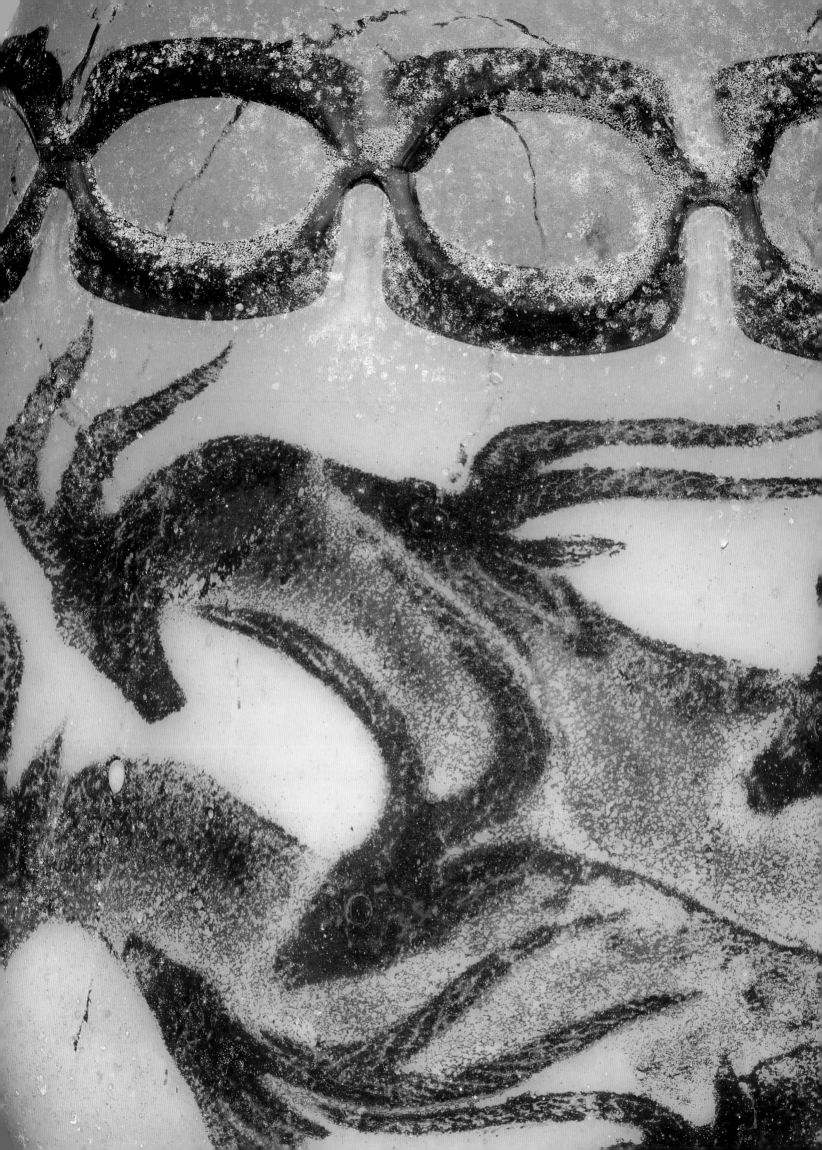

*Left and right:*
**Suspended Artifact:**
**Braided Pouch with**
**Lashed Tusk, 1995**

And with those first combinations, suddenly Morris's work was asking more intricate versions of the questions he always had posed: What are these things doing together? How do these shapes, textures and colors relate? What do they signify?

The components he uses today are drawn from a dazzling roomful of "spare parts" across from his studio at Pilchuck Glass School: urns and batons, arrows and gourds, animal horns, animal masks, countless variations on the shape of a traditional African tribal scepter called an *orinka,* pouches and quivers, needles and spoons.

He tends to blow the pieces individually, rather than dwelling on some overall plan. He then works with various combinations suspended together until something emerges that strikes a chord. "Blowing the pieces and then putting them together are two different things. I end up basing a lot of faith on the components that I use, but invariably I know they [the final pieces] are not going to come out like I envision."

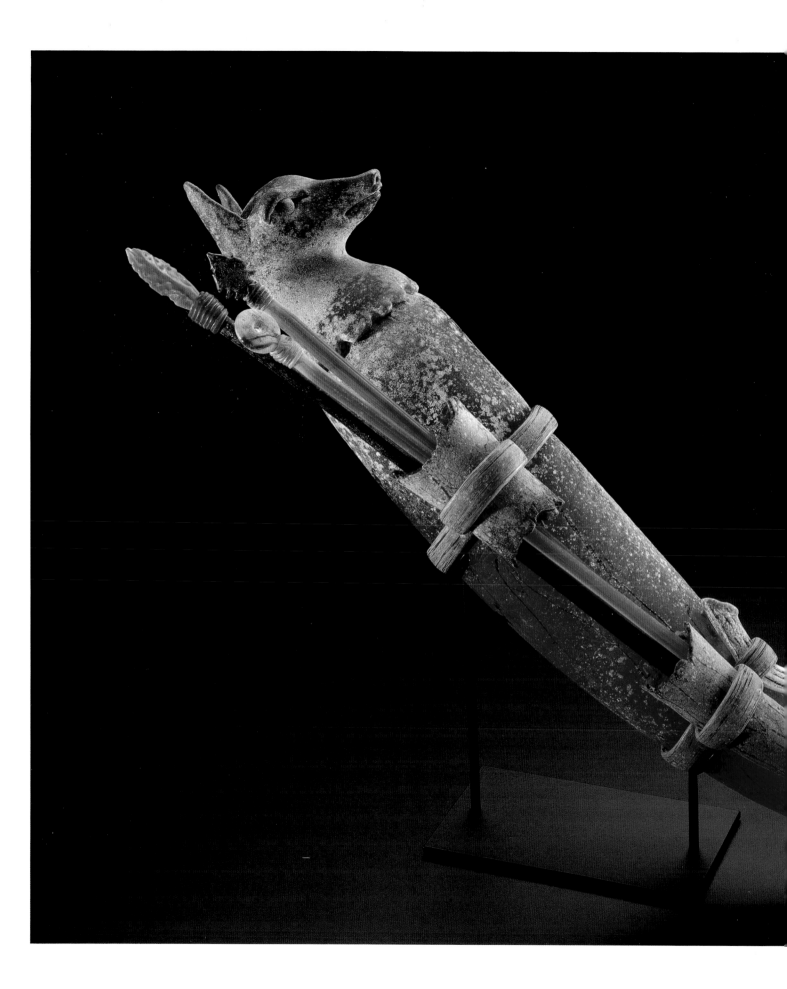

One group of artifacts that he experimented with ultimately grew to thirteen red, brown, and yellow *orinka*s and gourd shapes hung from a horizontal tusk. Another became an arrangement of tusks, antlers, and an animal-headed amulet. A third, reminiscent of the rafts, combined a gourd with a pouch bearing a skull inside, all hung from a spear shaft with a white crystalline tip.

With the recent addition of animal masks to the artifact groups, Morris has injected a new and arresting element to the series. He began to present the heads of animals as artistic components in his groupings, rather than just their surviving bones. A wolf mask might glare from the suspended collection, or the face of a deer, or the head of a sharp-beaked falcon. Clearly, they represent not the found objects of archaeology but something drawn either from mythic fantasy or the graphic reality of the trophy hunt.

As usual, Morris isn't offering up any explanations.

**Artifact Bundle: Fox,**
1995

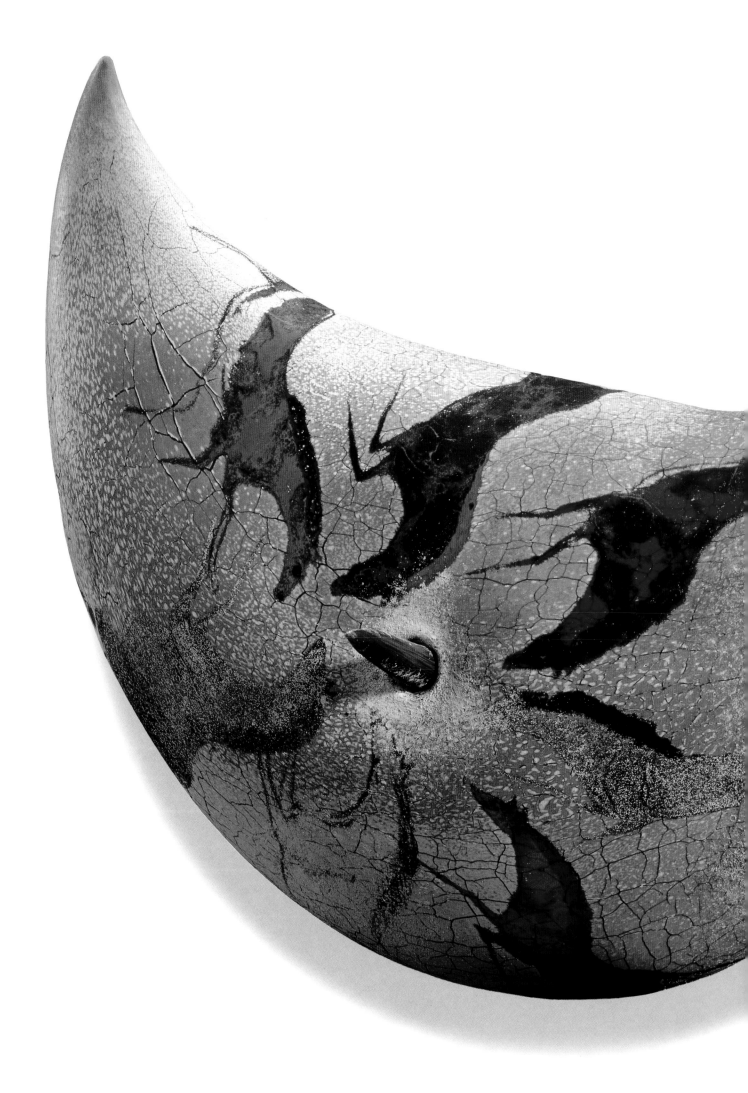

Parallel to the work with Suspended Artifacts, Morris has produced several series that make dramatic use of his longtime associate Jon Ormbrek's skills as a painter of figures in powdered glass. Three approaches—Artifact: Tooth; Artifact: Shard; and Artifact: Pouch—all present flat surfaces for Ormbrek's images, linking the ideas behind some of Morris's first decorated vessels with the more sophisticated interpretations of a prehistoric reality implicit in series titles like Tooth, Shard, and Pouch.

In Morris's lexicon, a Tooth is a big, heavy-looking piece, curved and tipped and fit for the jaw of something bigger than anyone has ever seen. On its broad face appears Ormbrek's drawing, often animal figures that strongly suggest the Cro-Magnon cave art of France and Spain.

Artifact: Tooth, 1994

Likewise, Morris's Shard is an expanse of textured glass pegged through with protruding stubs that altogether suggests a stretched hide, painted with the record of an oxen hunt or the ritualistic rendering of a group of horses.

In these pieces, and similar decorated versions of the Pouch series, Morris and Ormbrek present primitive man as artist himself, not just a tool-maker or weapon-wielder but as an incipient abstractionist, experimenting with the novel notion of capturing life in a two-dimensional image.

**Artifact: Shard with**
**Bone Pins, 1995**

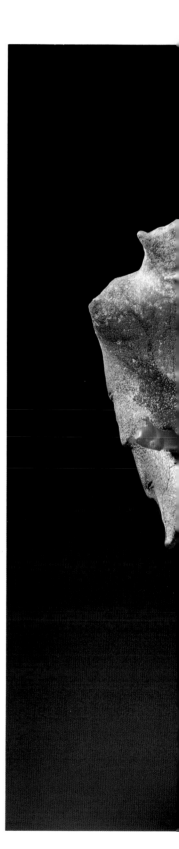

Artifact: Shard with
Bone Pins, 1995

Morris in effect has offered his surfaces
and Ormbrek's skilled hand to commem-
orate the emergence of those earliest
of all artists, and to remind modern humanity, distanced by millennia of accu-
mulated wisdom, sophistication, and
technology, of the images and ritual
needs that still can stir us all.

From Standing Stone to Artifact: Pouch,
Morris has traveled the millennia himself. Now, in the age of the Information
Superhighway, his art points down a
simpler path, where obsidian spear tips
are still there for the finding and serenity
lies not in solving the mysteries of life
but celebrating them.

**Artifact: Pouch, 1995**

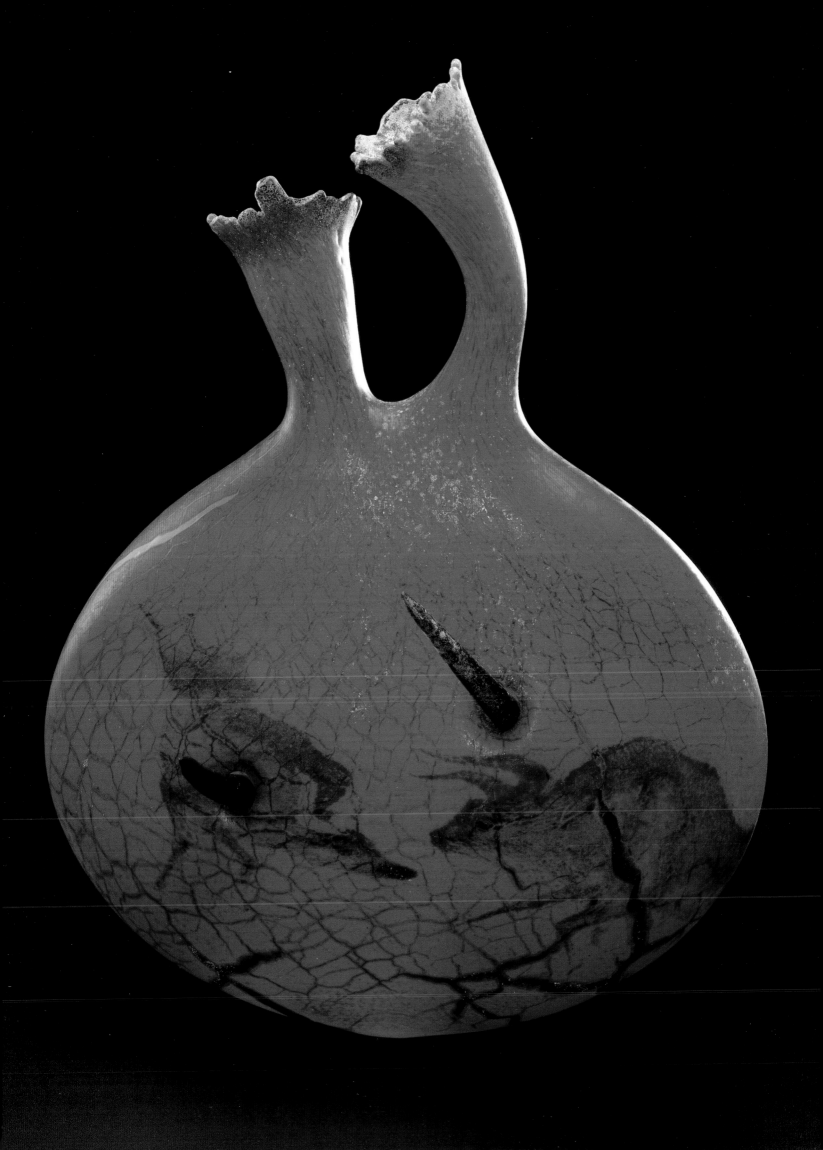

Suspended Artifact:
Braided Pouch, 1995

Suspended Artifact:
Tusk and Gourd, 1992

Suspended Artifact:
Braided Pouch, 1995

Suspended Artifact:
Pouch and Tusk, 1992

Artifact: Pouch, 1995

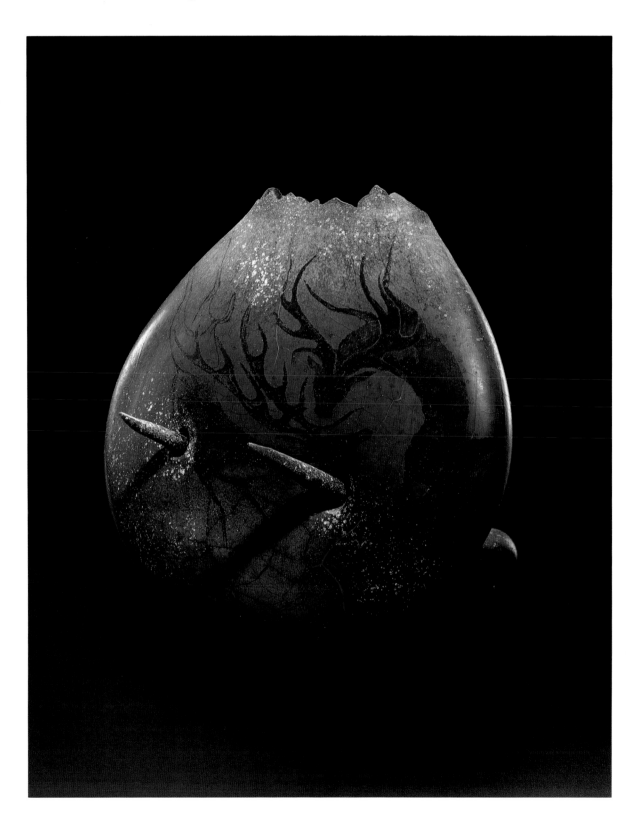

*Above and right:*
Garnering, 1990

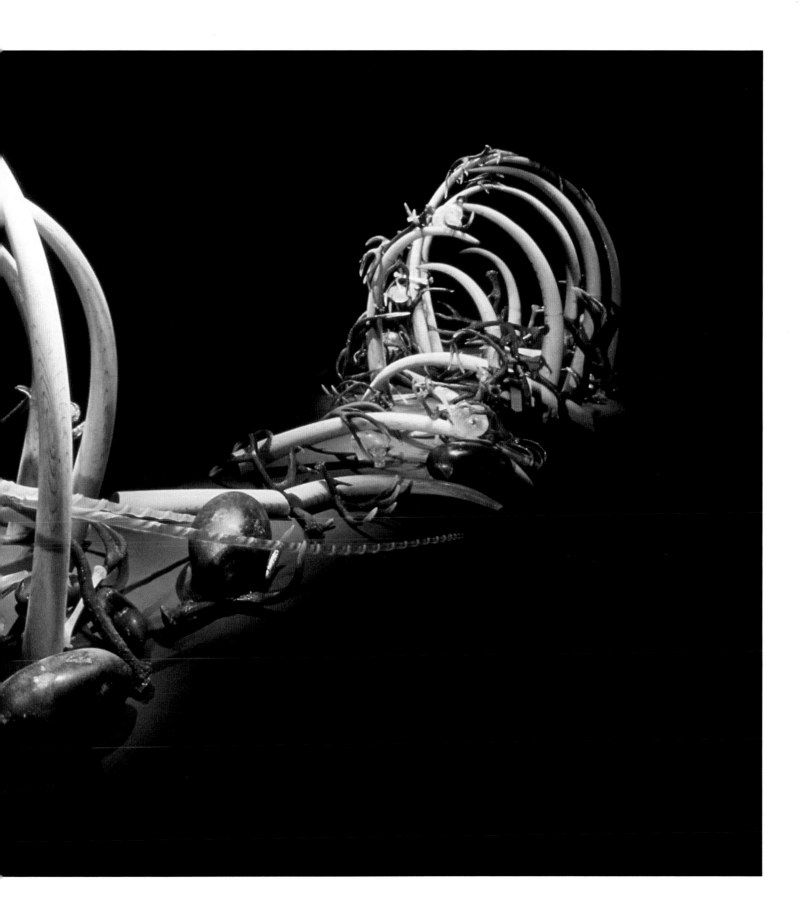

54

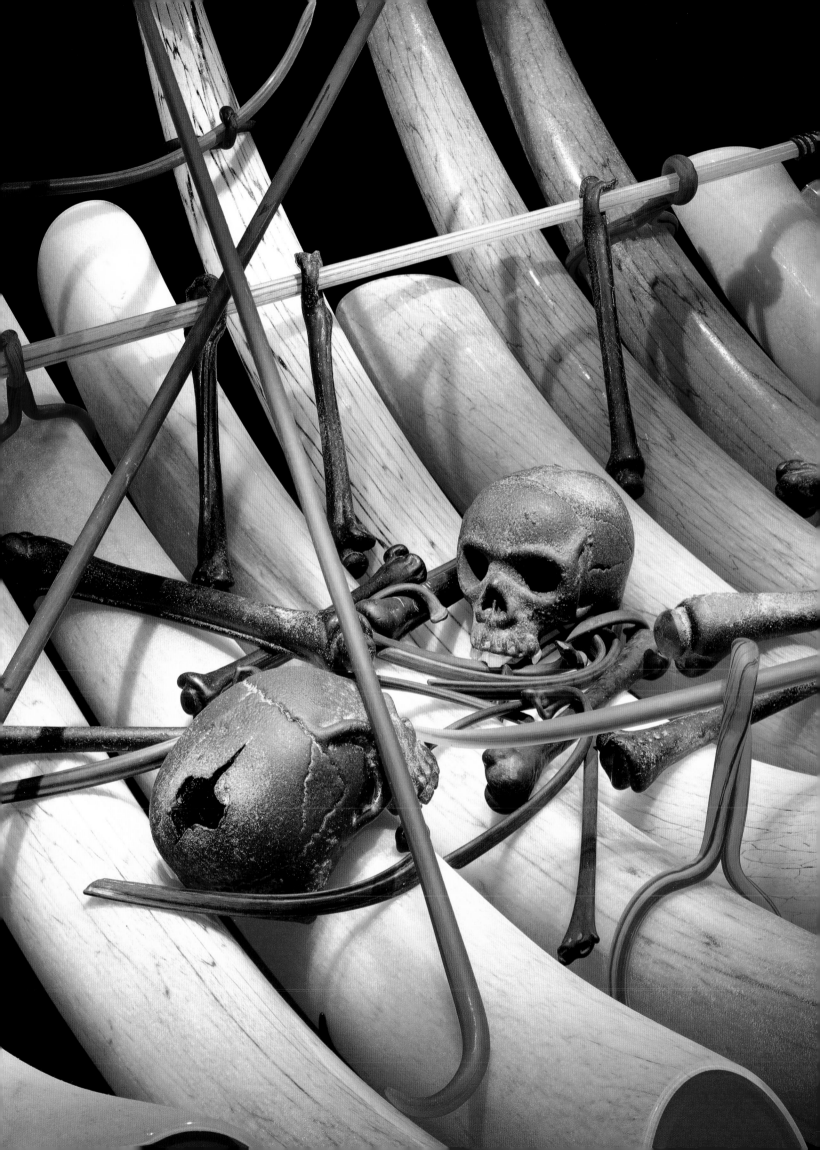

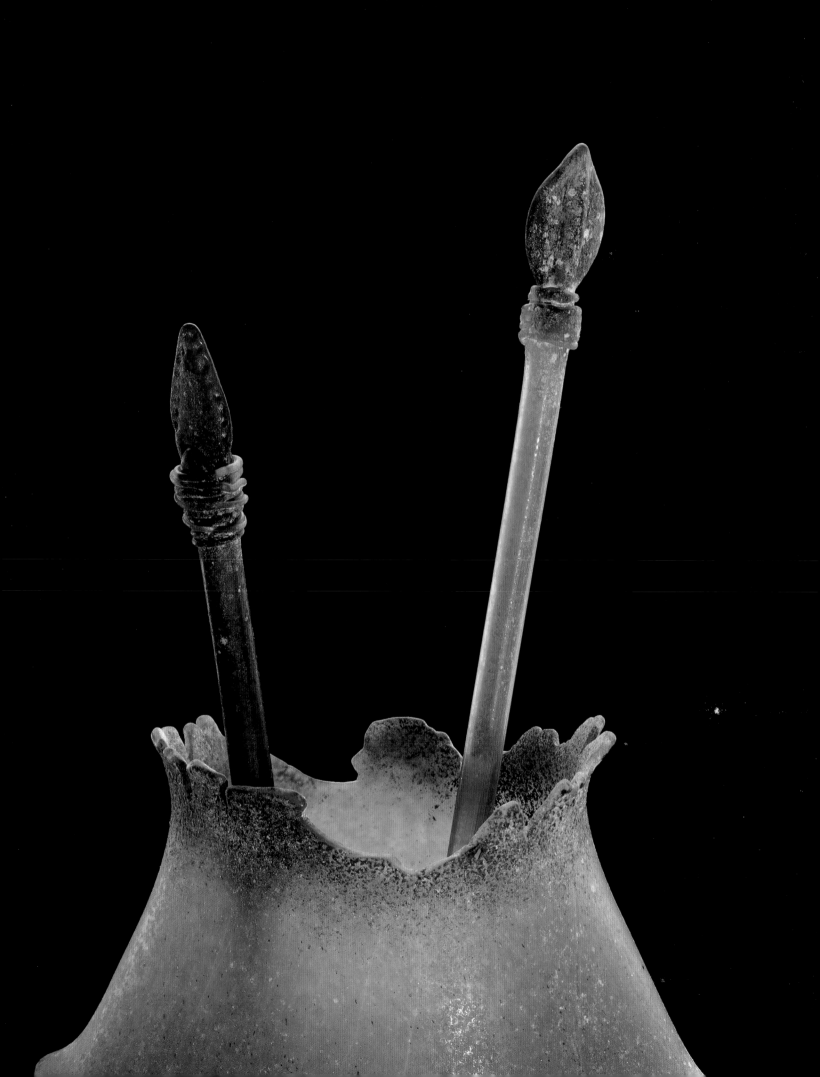

*Left and above:*
Suspended Artifact:
Pouch with Rhino
Horns, 1994

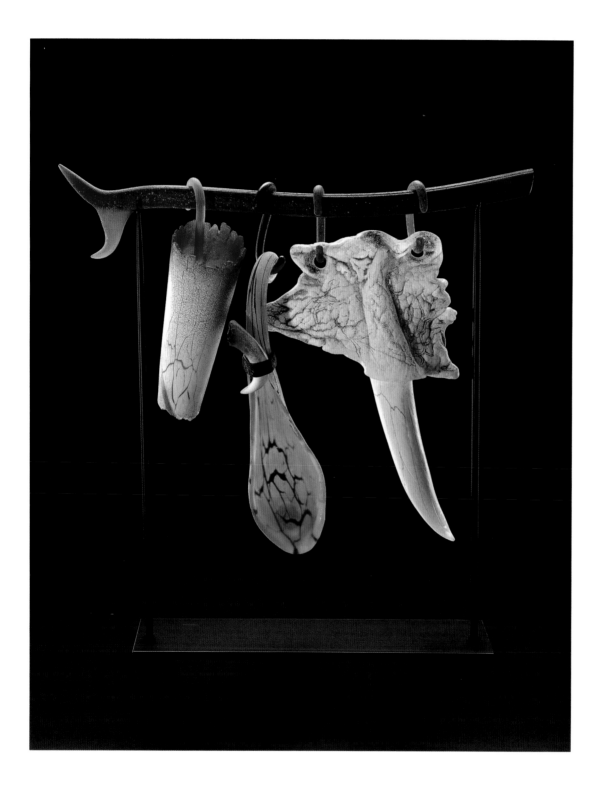

Suspended Artifact:
Walrus Tusk with
Scoop, 1995

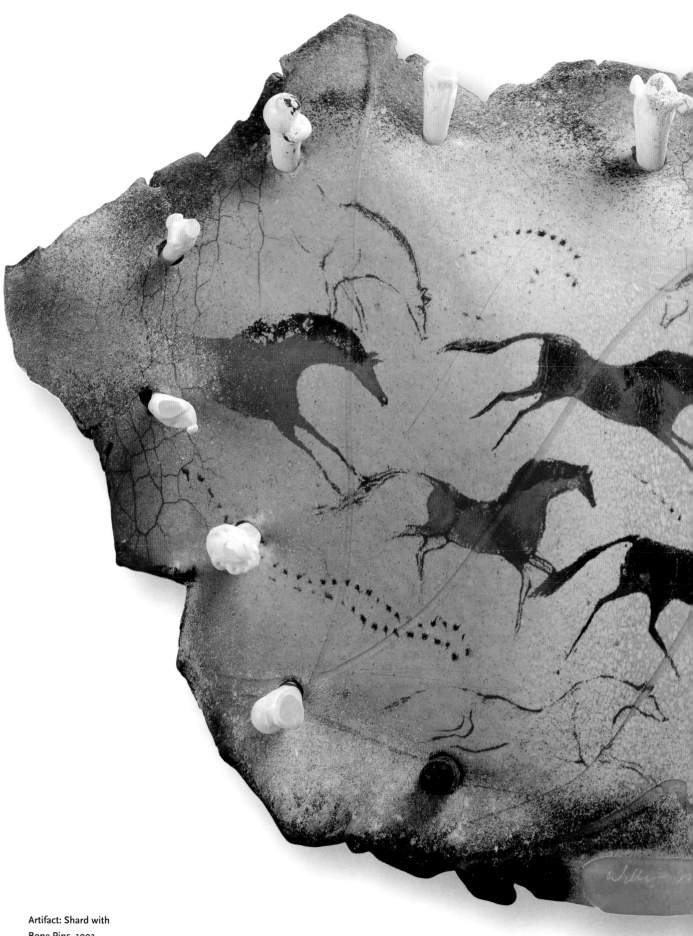

Artifact: Shard with
Bone Pins, 1993

Canopic Jar:
Pronghorn Antelope,
1993

Canopic Jar: Javan
Muntjac, 1994

Canopic Jars: Baboon
and Jackal, 1992

Canopic Jar: Red
Hawk, 1993

Artifact Bundles:
Ravens and Hawk,
1995

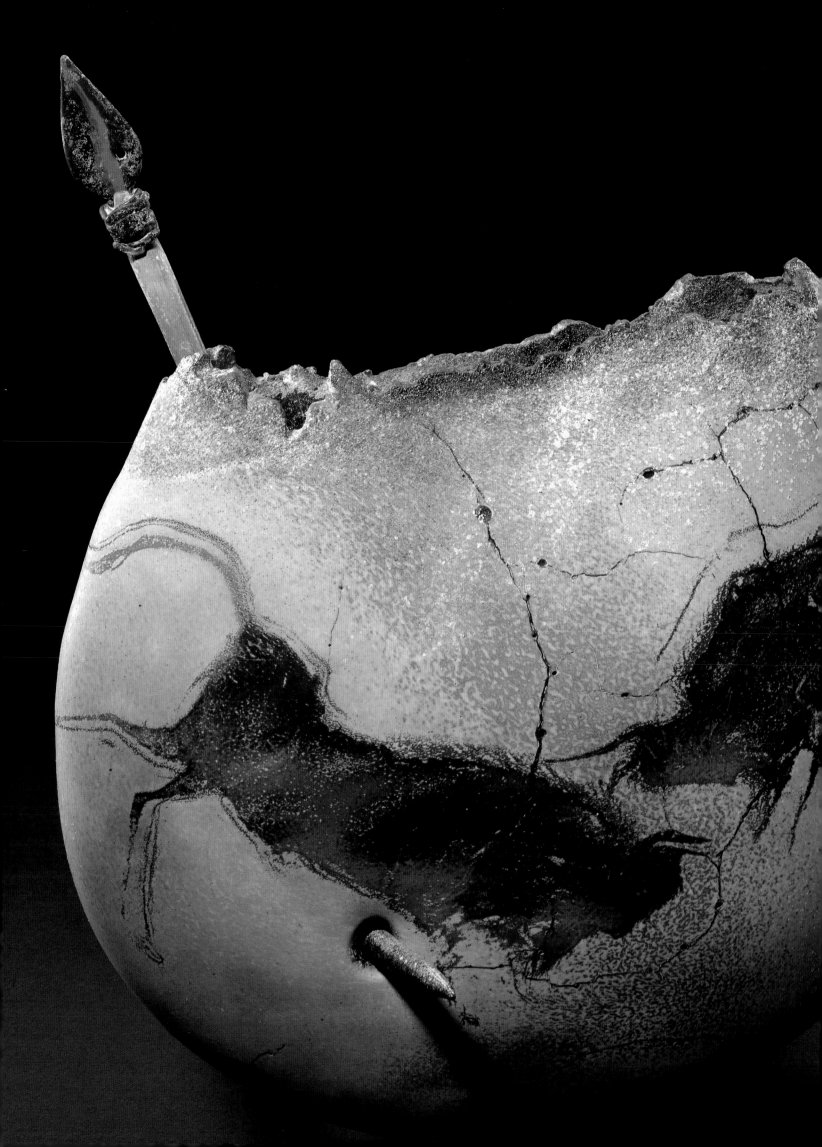

Artifact: Pouch, 1995

Detail, Artifact: Pouch,
1994

Artifact: Braided
Pouch, 1995

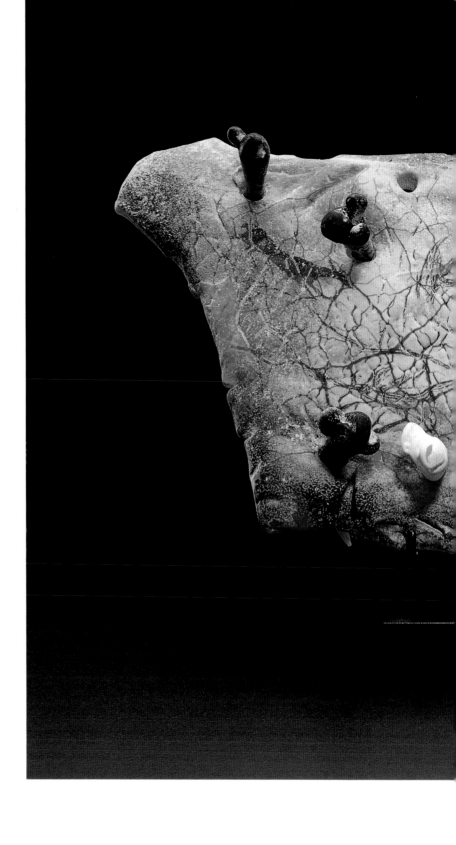

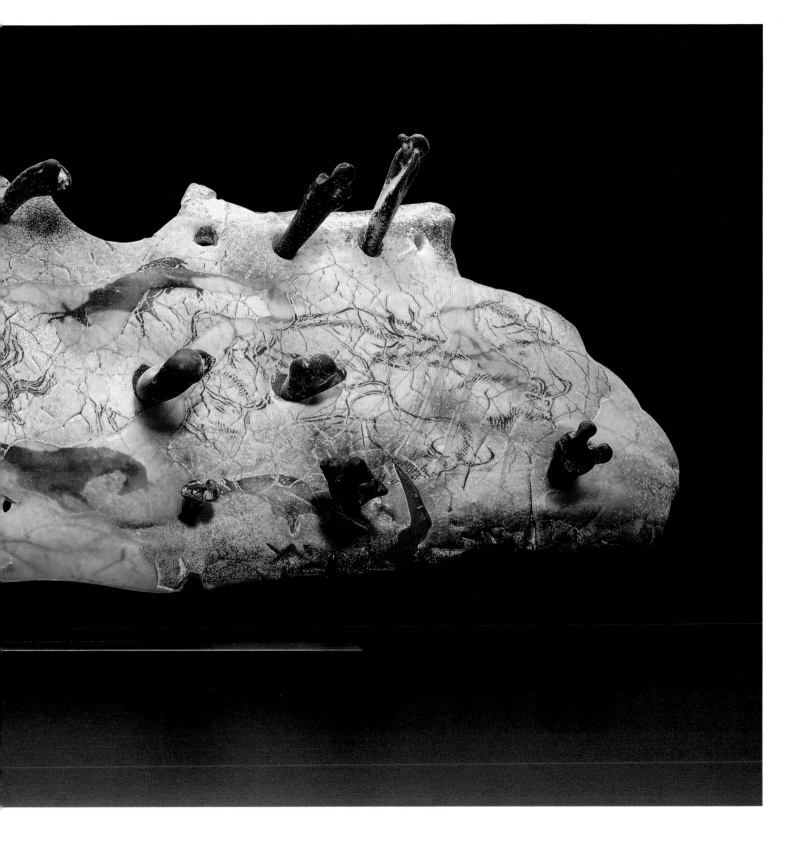

Artifact: Shard with
Bone Pins, 1994

Suspended Artifact:
Horned Vessel with
Antelope Skull, 1994

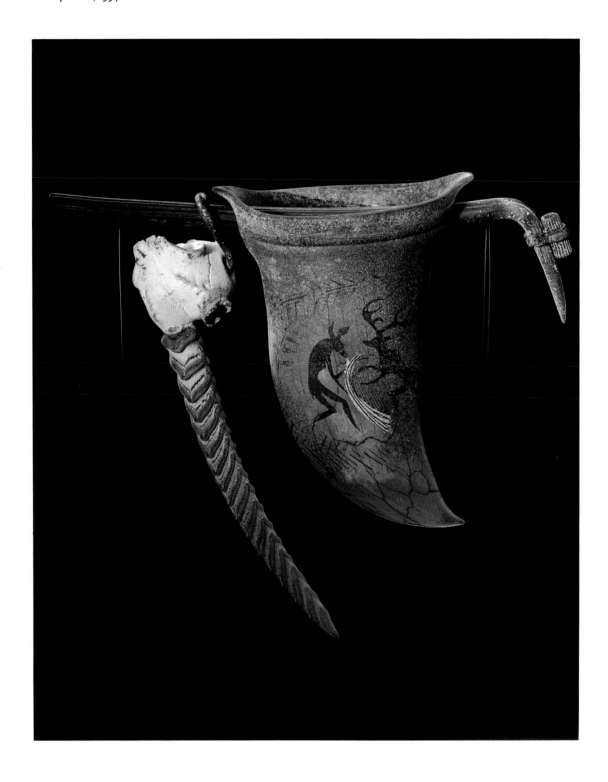

Detail, Suspended
Artifact: Walrus Tusk
with Wolf Mask and
Antler, 1995

Detail, Artifact Bundle:
Red Fox, 1995

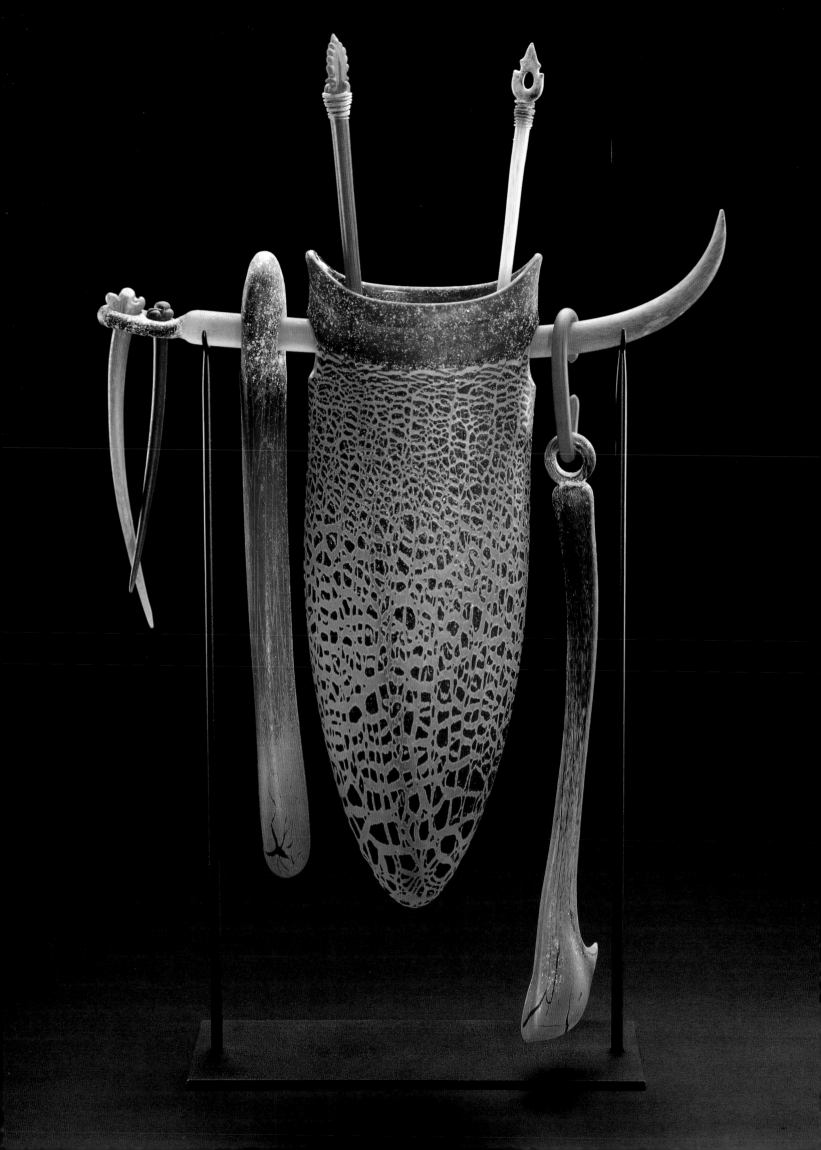

Suspended Artifact:
Pouch with Pins and
Orinka, 1993

Detail, Suspended
Artifact, 1995

Detail, Suspended
Artifact, 1995

Suspended Artifact:
Legged Pouch with
Rhino Horn, 1995

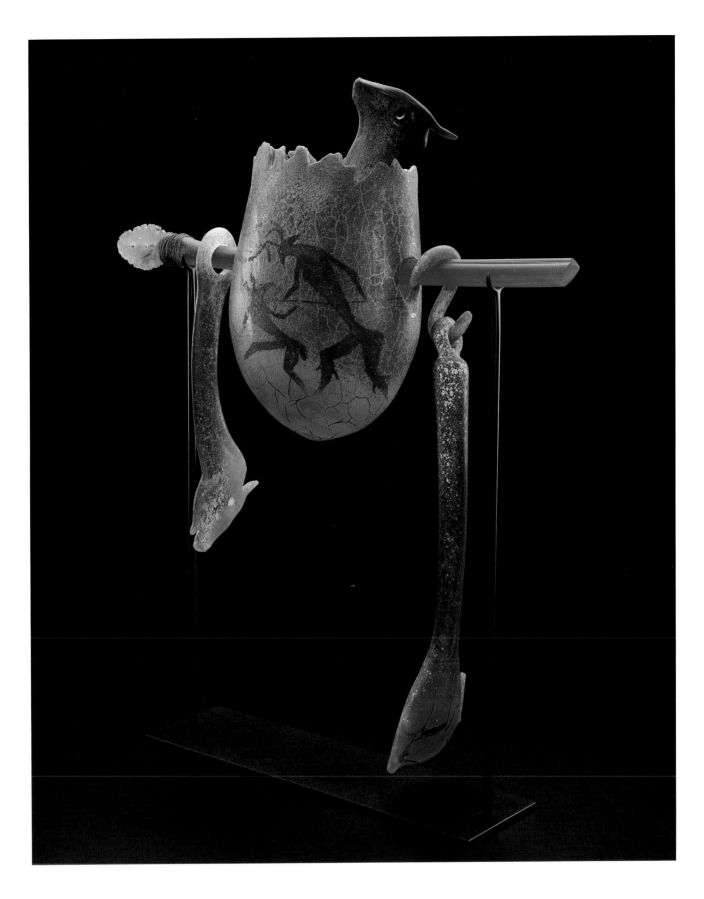

Suspended Artifact:
Pouch with Orinka
and Batons, 1993

*Above and right:*
Suspended Artifact:
Buffalo Pouch with
Orinka, 1995

Suspended Artifact:
Gourd with Rhino
Horns, 1995

Suspended Artifact:
Pouch with Tusks,
1993

Suspended Artifact:
Antler and Tusks, 1994

Detail, Suspended
Artifact, 1995

Suspended Artifact:
Quiver with Orinkas,
1993

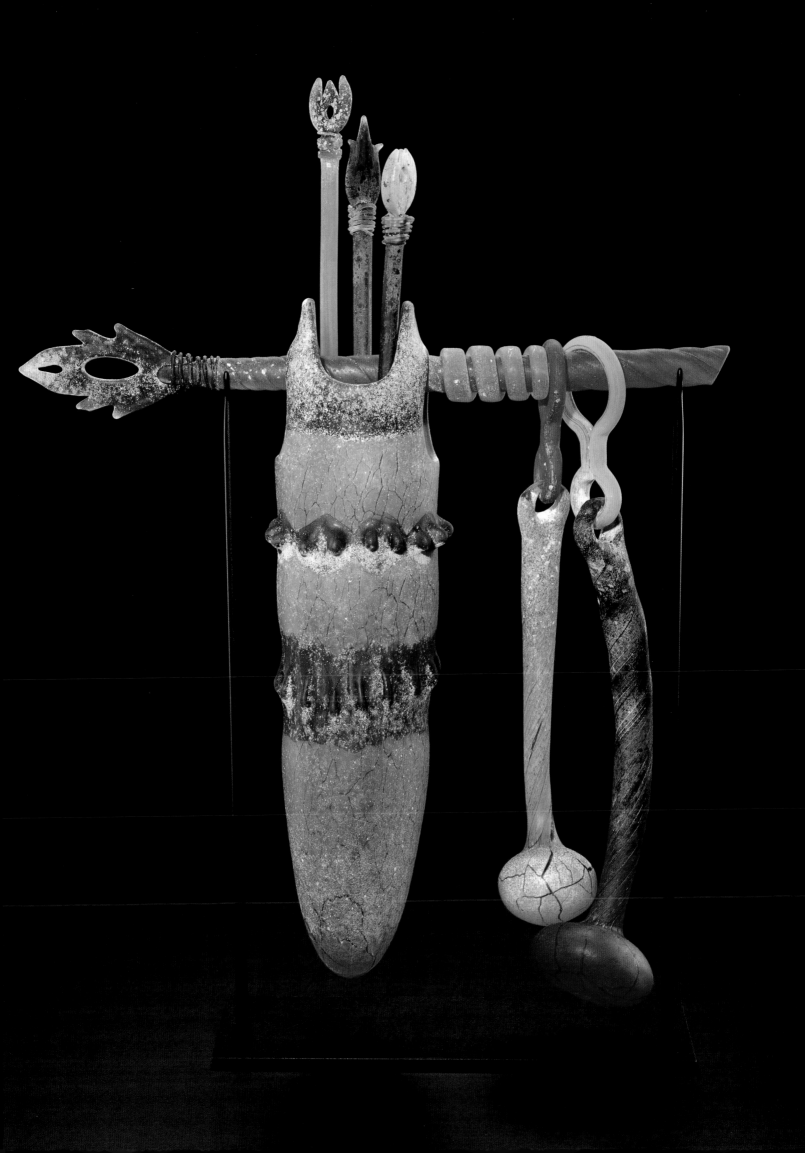

Canopic Jar:
Panther, 1992

Canopic Jar:
Hawk, 1992

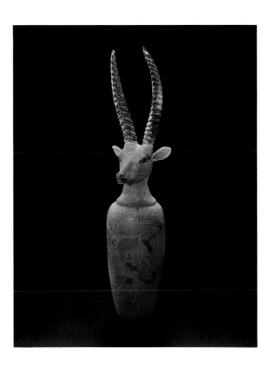

Canopic Jar:
Sable Antelope, 1995

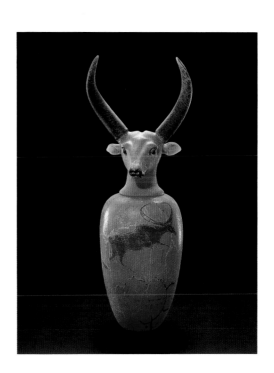

Canopic Jar:
African Bull, 1995

Canopic Jar:
Mountain Goat, 1992

Detail, Artifact
Bundles: Ravens, 1995

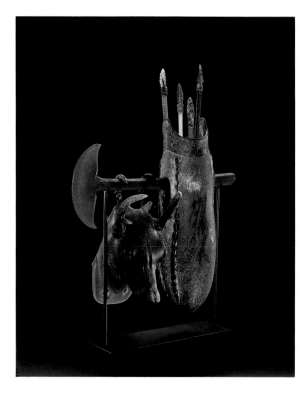

*Facing page:*
Suspended Artifact:
Raven Bundle and
Lashed Antler, 1995

Suspended Artifact:
Mask with Quiver,
1995

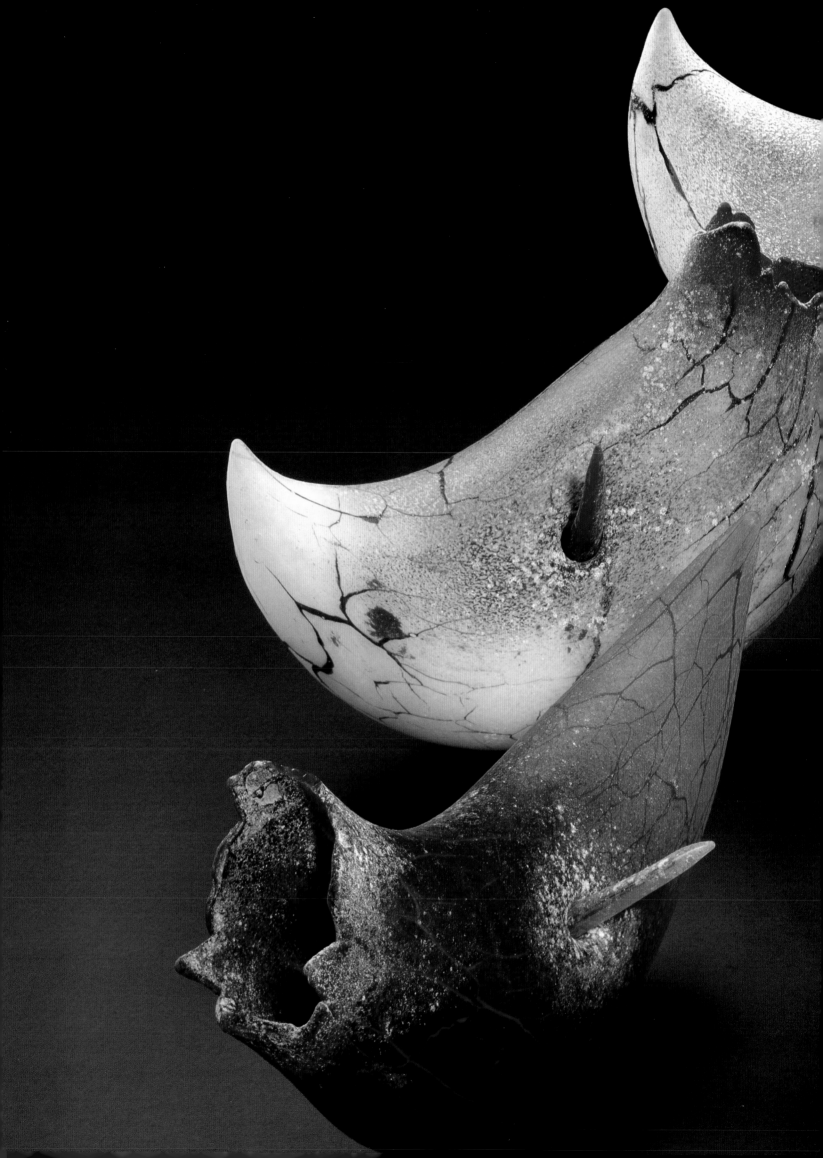

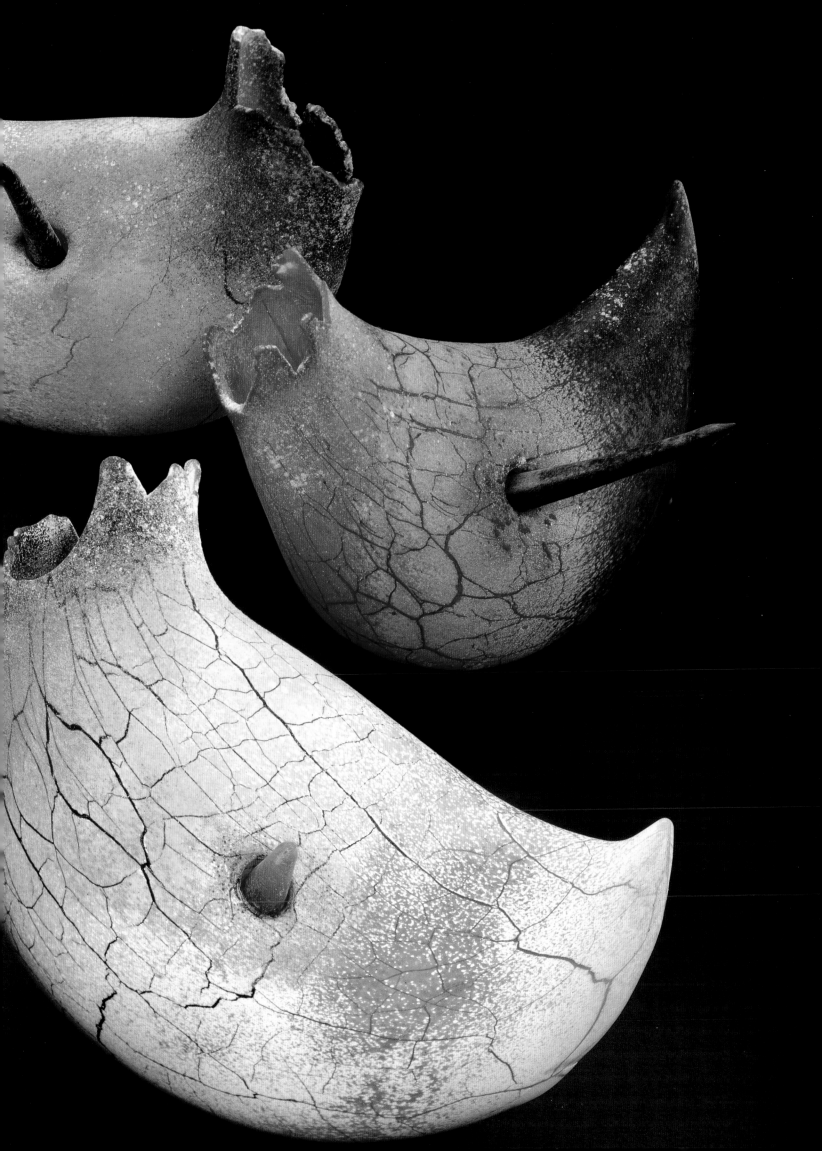

*Overleaf:* Grouping,
Artifact: Tooth, 1994

Artifact: Tooth, 1995

Artifact: Tooth, 1993

Artifact: Tooth, 1993

*Above and right:*
Suspended Artifact:
Pouch with Lashed
Scoop, 1995

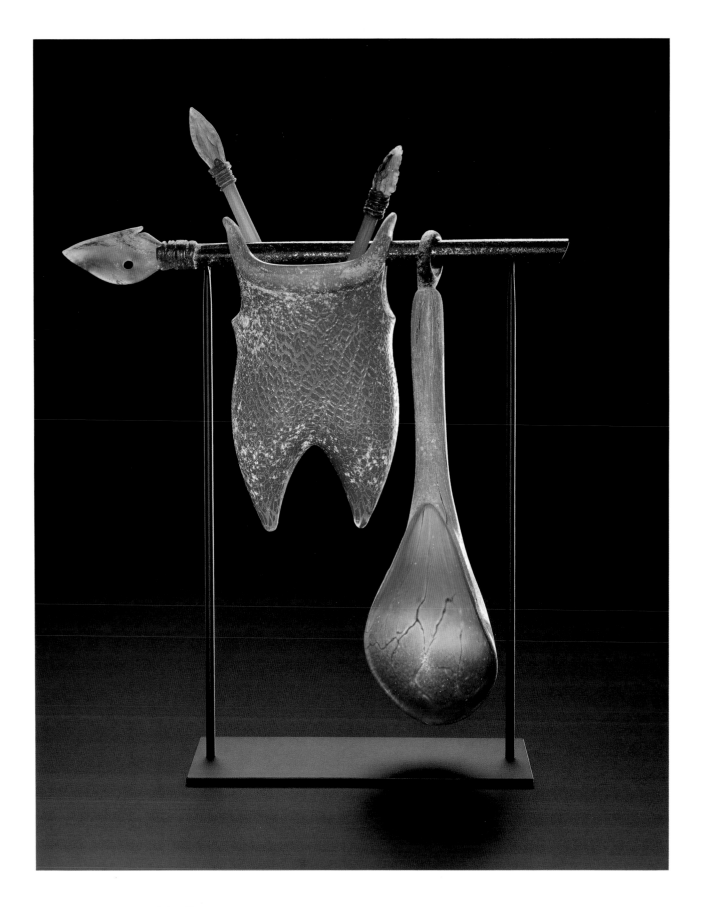

Suspended Artifact:
Scoop with Legged
Pouch, 1995

Suspended Artifact:
Baleen and Walrus
Tusk, 1995

*Above and right:* Suspended
Artifact: Horn Scoops with
Lashed Antler, 1995

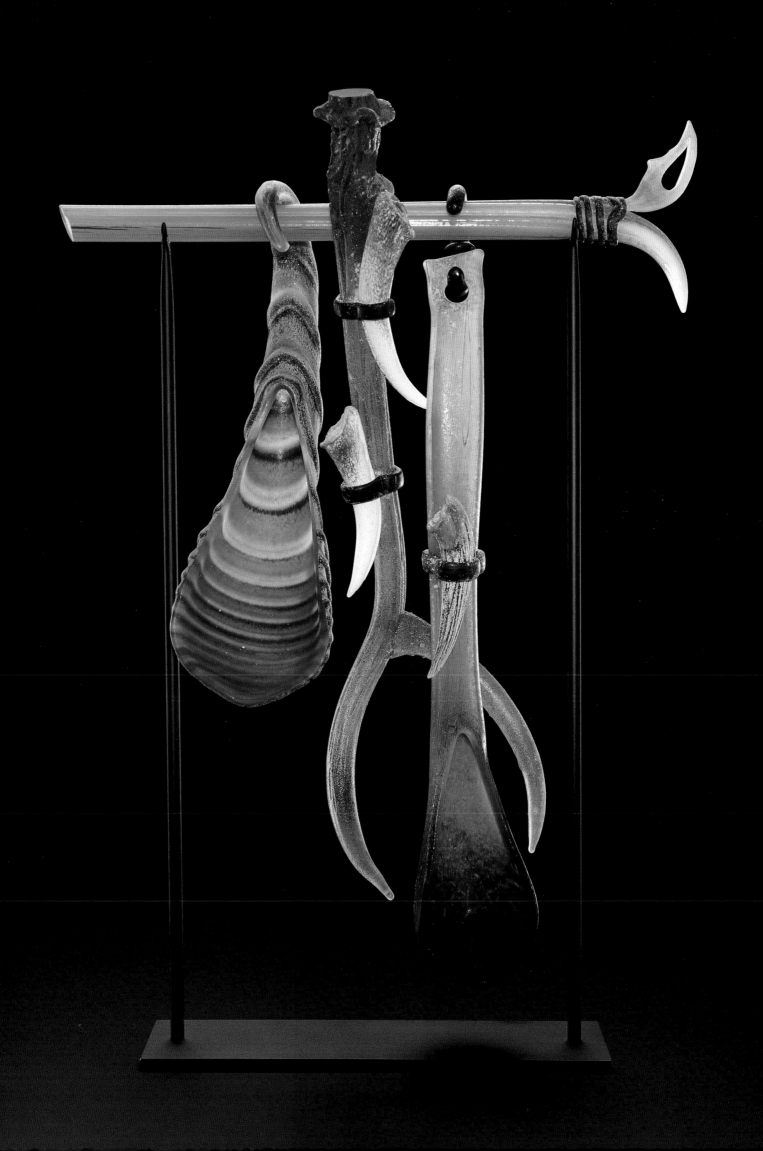

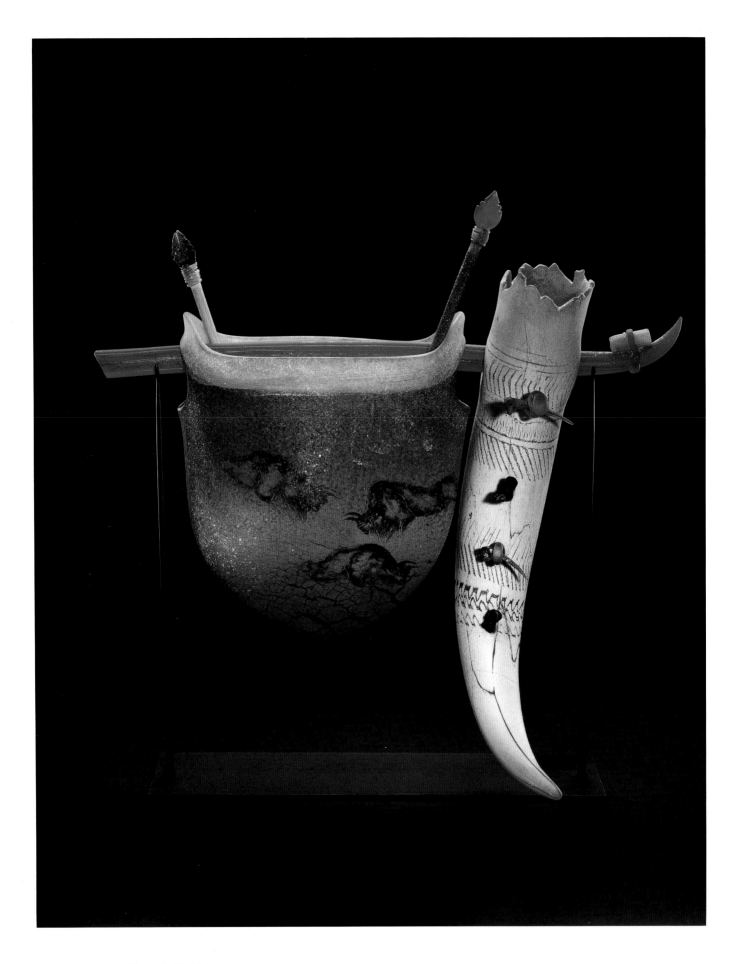

**Suspended Artifact:**
**Pouch with Tusk and**
**Bone Pins, 1994**

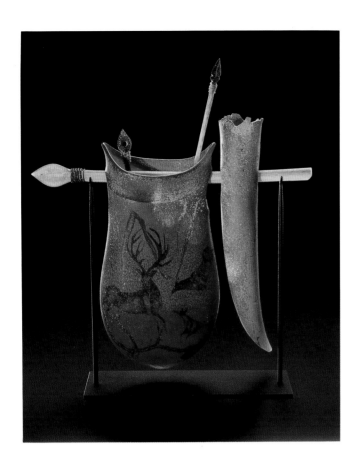

Suspended Artifact:
Pouch with Tusk, 1994

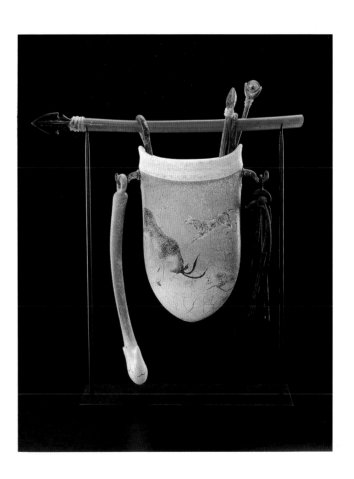

Suspended Artifact:
Pouch with Orinka,
1993

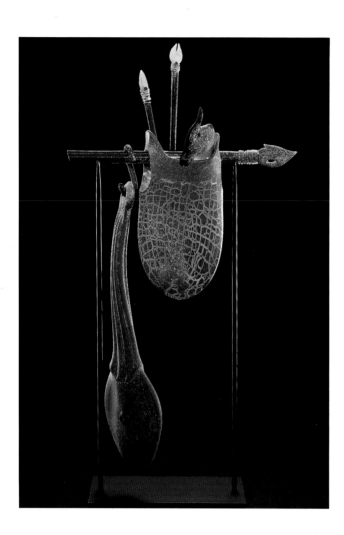

Suspended Artifact:
Pouch with Baton,
1995

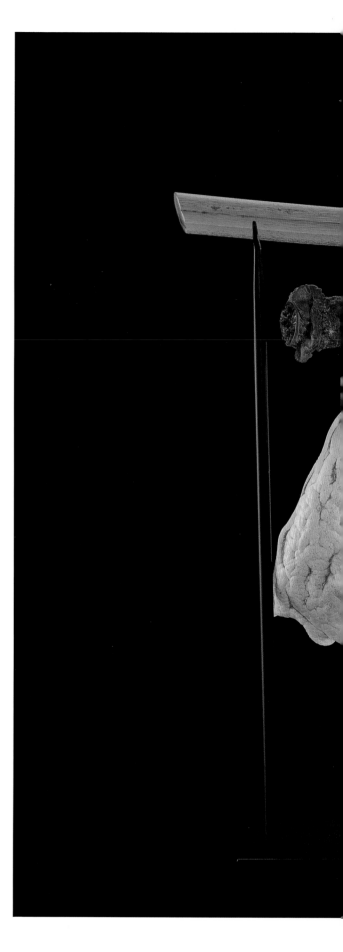

Suspended Artifact:
Walrus Tusk with
Lashed Antler, 1995

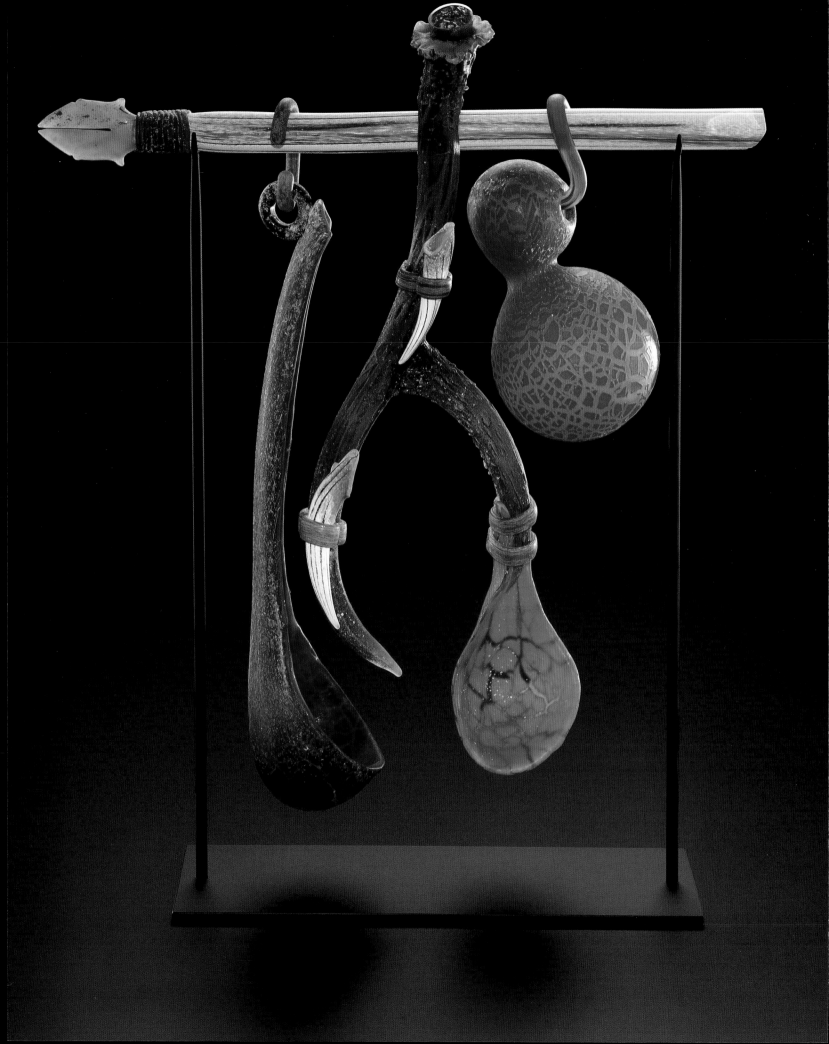

*Left and right:*
Suspended Artifact:
Antlered Spoon with
Scoop and Gourd,
1995

Suspended Artifact:
Scoop with Lashed
Antler and Tusks, 1995

Suspended Artifact:
Raven Mask with
Antlered Spoon and
Rhino Horn, 1995

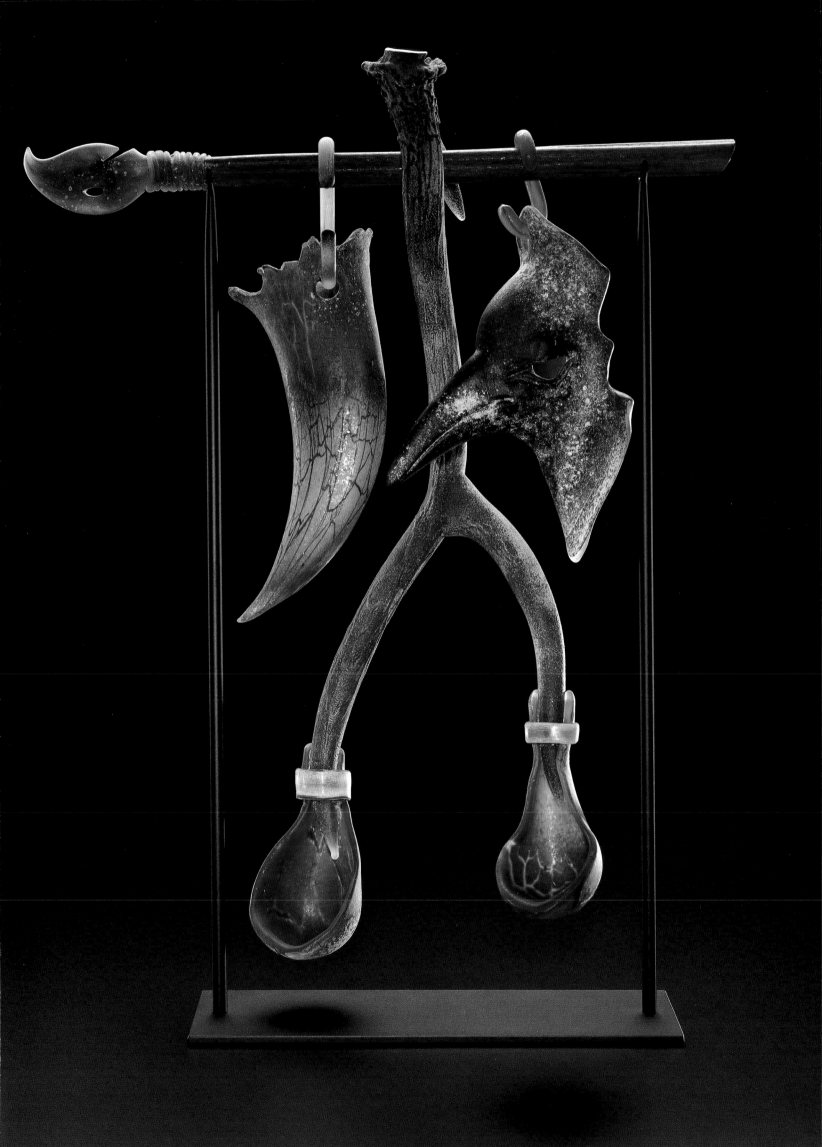

# STUDIO

A GLASSBLOWING STUDIO is an unadorned, roughed-up sort of place, more fit for a blacksmith than an artist. The tools are blowtorches and heavy black pincers, charred wooden paddles and fireproof gloves. But when an accomplished glassblower's team is at work—and accomplished glassblowing usually requires a team—the studio can become such a fluid blend of art and industry that the work seems less chore than choreography. Eyes always on the glass, working with near-silent, almost telepathic synchrony, William Morris and his crew move from oven to workbench to oven and back in a familiar ritual, gradually coaxing the glass from glowing ball into animal head or weapon or horn. It is a dance, and at its best it is so hypnotic that one tends to forget the dominant fact that underlies all else in this busy room: the glass is very, very hot.

Assorted tools

To remain workable through a process that can last as long as six or seven uninterrupted hours, the emerging work must be maintained at about 1,700 degrees Farenheit—so hot that it ignites wood on contact, so plastic and willful that if it is not kept in constant, centrifugal motion, gravity will take over and art will imitate molasses. Whatever else a glassblower is doing, the relentless rotation of the pipe can never stop for very long, and neither can the constant "flashing," the reheating of the glass in the roaring "glory hole" of the oven.

Heat, gravity, motion, simple tools. Coupled with the technical knowledge of a pyro-chemist and the precision of a sculptor, they are the stuff that turns sand to artwork.

Morris sculpting
fox head

Reheating antler in
glory hole

Hand torch

It all begins with sand, of course, and what sand it is—mixed with manganese dioxide and fluorspar and lithium carbonate and antimony oxide so it will stay optimally soft and malleable, and pelletized so its dust doesn't eventually suffocate its users. By the hundreds of pounds on busy days, the pellets are dumped into a glass-melting furnace heated to 2,450 degrees. The compound melts yellow-white, a gelatinous mass the color of sun.

Stand near the ovens or beside the crew's blowtorches, and it becomes clear that, say, four o'clock on a July afternoon would not be the best time to blow glass. So the Morris team— Morris, Randy Walker, Karen Willenbrink, and Jon Ormbrek—works early and only in cool seasons, beneath the high, octagonal roof of the open-sided and essentially outdoor studio of Pilchuck Glass School. The school where Morris got his start is closed in winter, so he rents it for the off-season. Virtually all of Morris's art is made here, in the woods of northwest Washington amid the log buildings of this most famous of all American glass academies. On blustery days, the wind swirls past the ad hoc plastic drapes hanging along the open sides of the studio, and sometimes the snow blows in, too. The weather, the setting, the architecture are all rustic and slightly wild, appropriate to what the artists inside are all about.

Morris reheating at
glory hole

Randy Walker is a former Oklahoma construction worker in his mid-thirties who stumbled into glassblowing, attended Pilchuck Glass School in 1991, "stuck and never went home." Now he is Morris's chief assistant, a serious, quietly intense technician of glass and Morris's running partner when the work is over.

Karen Willenbrink is a perennially cheerful Ohioan who took glassblowing as an elective at Ohio University and was hooked. Now in her mid-thirties, she has worked for Morris for eight years, and when she isn't either helping with the project at hand or crafting arrows, spearheads, hanging hooks, and other small items to complete his assemblages, she spends weekends fashioning delicate glass flowers, as different from weapons and bones as art can be.

Walker and Willenbrink are Morris's extra hands and eyes, constantly attentive to the work before them. They are as quick and involved as a surgical team, which sometimes they seem to be as they pass Morris tools, prepare space for his next steps, and position wooden paddles between his bare hands and the hot glass to protect him from burns when he is working at close quarters.

Much of what they do is the same work as any glassblowing team, even though Morris's unusual work often demands unusual techniques and endurance. But there is a third member of the team who does something quite unlike anyone else in the world of studio glass. He is Jon Ormbrek, a bearded, crinkly-eyed native Washingtonian, and what he does is create the faux-primitive drawings that adorn so much of Morris's glass.

*Overleaf:* Team at work; left to right: Walker, Ormbrek, Morris, Willenbrink

Ormbrek has worked with Morris since they met at Central Washington University in 1977, and in that time he has developed his own method and style of glass decoration, much akin to Native American sand painting. Using finely powdered, colored glass, he sprinkles and shapes his designs on smooth metal plates. When the powdered glass art and its plate are heated, and Morris rolls a glowing-hot glass shape over the design, the images transfer to the artwork like reverse fingerprints.

**Walker puntying bundle with team at work**

Once embedded in the glass, the animals or hunters or other figures stretch and grow, changing form and attitude with the changing shape and size of the developing art. Watching a tiny, simple figure gradually become a large and mysterious image on the face of the glass is a magical experience, but Ormbrek shares Morris's comfortable vagueness about what it is he does and where the ideas come from.

"What makes art art and not just technique? I could never pin that down," he says. He chews on that thought a moment and then says with the slightest twinkle in his eye: "If you could pin it down in words, there'd be no point in making this stuff."

Ormbrek with sand
drawing

However casually Ormbrek and Morris talk about their creations, though, there is nothing casual or easy about what the Morris glass artists do. That becomes dramatically apparent during one typical morning in the studio. Morris and company have spent more than an hour fashioning a curved, two-foot-long, tapering form that suggests something between tusk and tooth, coated with white glass dust, its surface webbed with burgundy veins. It is elegant and lethal-looking, but the moment has come when it must be transferred to a new pipe, and suddenly it seems dangerously vulnerable and fragile.

The exchange of an object from one blowpipe to another is a common glass-blowing procedure that allows the opening where the original pipe held the glass to be shaped and finished. Absent the heat, such a shift of grips would be as simple as changing hands, but at 1,700 degrees, simple it is not.

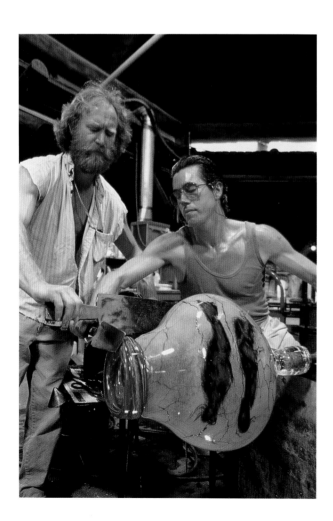

Ormbrek and Morris
at work

Walker tips a new pipe with a hot button of glass and sticks it onto the tusk, opposite the point where the original pipe is attached. It bonds in seconds. Then he and Morris use water to quick-cool the old pipe joint so that a gentle tap can break it free.

Morris administers the tap. The tusk separates from the pipe. In fact it separates from both pipes—and smashes on the cement floor.

There is silence.

Willenbrink looks away. Walker's shoulders drop. Morris mutters, paces a circle, swears a little, then remembers he has a visitor.

He gestures elaborately at the shattered glass. "That NEVER happens!" he says with a stagy scowl.

"Right," says Walker, "and we have a whole landfill out back to prove it."

The second most important fact of a glassblowing studio, after the heat, is that glass breaks. And the more intricate and painstaking the process that came before, the harder it is to look at those angry fragments on the concrete that had come so close to being something wonderful. Glassblowers call them "floor models."

For every piece of glass standing resplendent in a museum, gallery, or collector's home, there are the floor models, the accidents, miscalculations of heat or timing, misjudgments about the thickness of a surface that has cracked or the temperature of a quick-cooling protrusion that has snapped off. There is no way to fix it. There is only starting over, and grappling once again with the only artistic medium that actively fights back.

Ormbrek, Willenbrink,
and Morris torching
antler and tusk

Sculpting antler tine

A sculptor's marble block just stands there; so does a painter's canvas. But glass tries to flee, refuses to obey, remembers every mistake. Always its accomplice is gravity, tugging away at an artist's best intentions. Everything a glassblower does—and the individual steps to create one piece can number in the hundreds—is aimed at subduing the natural inclinations of gravity and glass.

The process is called glassblowing, but in the nature of Morris's work, very little literal glassblowing occurs. He usually puffs into the pipe only a few times at the beginning of his work, to form a thick-skinned bubble. Then he rolls, squeezes, pushes and pulls that bubble, heating and cooling and coating and dusting it until, gradually, it takes on the proportions and detail of finished art.

On another, more successful day in the studio, Morris goes about sculpting the head of a deer for the lid of a canopic jar, a form inspired by Egyptian burial vessels. His work is a wonder to watch:

At first the glass seems heavy, thick, and resistant to change as it cools on the pipe from near-liquid white to jellied

Morris quenching
glass

orange in the first moments out of the furnace. But change it does, first gradually as Morris dusts it with a new coating of powdered glass, then abruptly and in a dramatic fashion as he plunges it into a pail of water. Steam erupts to the ceiling, Morris disappears in the cloud, and the glass hisses explosively. As the steam fades, the glass emerges transformed, its surface shattered into a spiderweb crackle by the temperature difference between the hot ball and its cooler outer layer.

Then comes the reason for the steam treatment: Morris fills the cracks with dark glass powder that will produce marbled veins of color in the finished work. They will suggest great age and stress—trademarks of Morris's work.

The piece already is becoming something of startling beauty, but this is going to be a deer head in the end, and so the next hours will be spent gradually and patiently persuading that graceful animal head into being.

Morris sculpting
fox head

Morris pulling an ear

Morris measuring
for horn

Applying glass powder
to Canopic Jar head

Whether the art in process is a deer head, merely an antler, or something as exotic as a long, flat piece of whale baleen, the shapes are sculpted with the most humdrum of tools—pliers, shears, tweezers, long and pointed grasping and shaping instruments called jacks, paddles, metal rods, wooden dowels, gloved hands, gravity.

Morris uses them all on the deer, starting with tweezers. Gripping a piece of the top-left surface of the glass, he pulls a couple inches of near-molten glass out to form the first hint of an eye. He does it again at top right—another eye—and again in the middle of the glass ball—the nose. The ball of glass has begun to look like a clownish balloon head.

Tool by tool, step by step, the features slowly are drawn out of the smooth face of the glass: the crown of the head, a brow line, eye sockets, a delicate jaw. Observing the process is like watching an embryo take shape in time-lapse photography, interrupted every minute or two by a trip to the glory hole for reheating.

It is not all smooth, steady progress, though. Problems arise: proportions go awry as the glass is pulled and stretched; thin spots occur, dangerously fragile; the look of the face isn't quite right, a matter for consultation with the crew.

"Glassblowing is like relationships," Morris says with a grin. "It's not as important how good you are the first time as it is how well you fix your mistakes."

And so the deer head changes, improves, takes on an identity and a winsome expression, craft becoming art.

At points throughout the process, and especially near the end, Morris works the surface of the deer head with varied colors of powdered glass to gain the color shadings he wants, and with *scavo* (from the Italian word that means "to dig"), a compound that deglosses and roughens the surface when heated. These are the times when Morris the chemist is most evident, and when the uniqueness of his art is most apparent.

But after hours of painstaking work on the deer's gentle face, the application of the *scavo* seems almost an act of destruction. The deer head is suddenly no longer a thing of beauty. The surface has turned a scabrous, bumpy yellow and brown. This looks like a terrible mistake.

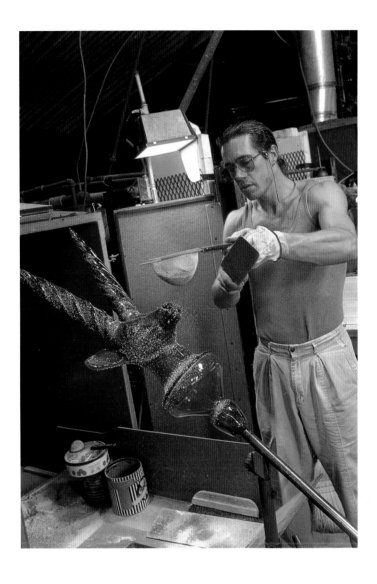

Applying *scavo* to
Canopic Jar head

Reheating Canopic
Jar head

Nevertheless, the sculpture is complete, and with a final tap on the pipe, the head breaks free and drops into Walker's arms. He is wearing heavy gloves and a silvery, heavily insulated and padded jacket especially made for those moments when the glass is carried from the workbench to an annealing oven for slow cooling.

A new smell wafts through the room, the smell of his burning gloves. That familiar aroma signals that the piece is done for the moment. After hours or days have passed, when the work is hard and cold, the infernal *scavo* crust will be washed off, revealing the marvelously textured surface it has created underneath. Any remnant glass protrusions will be ground away, and the surface treated with hydrochloric acid to eliminate any surviving glassy gleam.

Then the piece truly will be finished. In this case, the deer-capped burial urn is a special commission, one of three ordered by a Morris admirer who eventually foresees them being used as, yes, burial urns.

Watching a fine glassblower go through such a project is a revelation. Being a fine glassblower, Morris says, also has its moments.

"It's an education for me, too," he says. "Sometimes I'm just along for the ride. There's no way to write a manual for this."

*Below left:* Reheating Canopic Jar head

Morris with finished
Canopic Jar head

*Overleaf*:
Canopic Jar: Defassa
Water Buck, 1994

127

# LIST OF ILLUSTRATIONS

Unless otherwise indicated all dimensions are in inches; height precedes width precedes depth.

Pages 40–41
*Artifact Bundle: Fox*, 1995. 22 x 28 x 8. Private collection (A595.01.05).

Pages 42–43
*Artifact: Tooth*, 1994. 14 x 20 x 16. Collection of David Austin and Leisa J. Neal (AT594.03.02).

Page 44
*Artifact: Shard with Bone Pins*, 1995. 17 x 26 x 9. Collection of the artist (AS295.01.18).

Pages 44–45
*Artifact: Shard with Bone Pins*, 1995. 18 x 28 x 10. Private collection (AS595.01.15).

Page 47
*Artifact: Pouch*, 1995. 21 x 16 x 11. Private collection (AP295.01.03).

Page 48
*Suspended Artifact: Braided Pouch*, 1995. 29 x 27 x 7. Collection of Kirby and Priscilla Smith (SA595.09.06).

Page 49, top
*Suspended Artifact: Tusk and Gourd*, 1992. 28 x 24 x 9. Permanent Collection, Seattle Art Museum (SA392.25.05).

Page 49, bottom
*Suspended Artifact: Pouch and Tusk*, 1992. 23 x 20 x 8. Private collection (SA392.42.05).

Page 50
*Artifact: Pouch*, 1995. 16 x 17 x 14. Private collection (AP395.03.03).

Page 51
Detail, *Suspended Artifact*, 1994. Collection of Mr. and Mrs. Jack Robinson (SA1294.01.04).

Pages 52–53
*Garnering*, 1990. 7 x 25 x 9 feet. Installation, Renwick Gallery, Smithsonian Institution, Washington, D.C., December 14, 1990–September 15, 1991.

Pages 54 and 55 (detail)
*Cache*, 1993. 5 x 6 x 36 feet. Installation, American Craft Museum, New York, April 15–July 4, 1993.

Pages 56 (detail) and 57
*Suspended Artifact: Pouch with Rhino Horns*, 1994. 34 x 26 x 6. Collection of the artist (SA1094.01.09).

Page 58
*Suspended Artifact: Walrus Tusk with Scoop*, 1995. 28 x 28 x 9. Private collection (SA295.04.09).

Page 59
*Suspended Artifact: Jackal Mask with Baleen and Gourd*, 1995. 40 x 28 x 13. Collection of Dorothy and George Saxe (SA595.08.11).

Pages 60–61
*Artifact: Shard with Bone Pins*, 1993. 16 x 25 x 8. Collection of Dr. and Mrs. Robert Aptekar (AS593.01.16).

Page 62
*Canopic Jar: Javan Muntjac*, 1994. 43 x 10. Private collection (CJ1094.01.02).

Page 63
*Canopic Jar: Pronghorn Antelope*, 1993. 38 x 12. Collection of Mr. and Mrs. Peter Carbonaro (CJ1293.03.02).

Page 64, top
*Canopic Jar: Red Hawk*, 1993. 30 x 10. Collection of Becky and Jack Benaroya (CJ393.03.02).

Page 64, bottom
*Artifact Bundles: Ravens and Hawk*, 1995. H. 19–21. Private collection (A595.04.02, A595.05.02, A595.03.02).

Page 65
*Canopic Jars: Baboon and Jackal*, 1992. H. 22–27. Collection of George R. Stroemple.

Page 66
Detail, *Artifact: Pouch*, 1994. 19 x 18 x 15. Private collection (AP594.06.04).

Page 67
*Artifact: Pouch*, 1995. 18 x 18 x 15. Private collection (AP595.02.05).

Page 68
*Artifact: Braided Pouch*, 1995. 17 x 17 x 12. Collection of the artist (AP595.01.04).

Pages 68–69
*Artifact: Shard with Bone Pins*, 1994. 17 x 23 x 8. Private collection (AS1294.02.19).

Page 70
*Suspended Artifact: Horned Vessel with Antelope Skull*, 1994. 24 x 28 x 10. Private collection (SA1294.06.05).

Page 71
*Suspended Artifact: Rhino Horns*, 1993. 27 x 23 x 8. Private collection (SA1093.04.05).

Page 72
Detail, *Suspended Artifact: Walrus Tusk with Wolf Mask and Antler*, 1995 (see page 8).

Pages 72–73
Detail, *Artifact Bundle: Red Fox*, 1995. Private collection (A595.02.05).

Page 74
*Suspended Artifact: Pouch with Pins and Orinka*, 1993. 37 x 24 x 5. Collection of the Corporate Office of Keith McCaw (SA1293.07.10).

Page 75, left
Detail, *Suspended Artifact*, 1995.

Page 75, right
Detail, *Suspended Artifact*, 1995 (see page 8).

Page 76
*Suspended Artifact: Legged Pouch with Rhino Horn*, 1995. 26 x 19 x 7. Private collection (SA595.15.06).

Page 77
*Suspended Artifact: Pouch with Orinka and Batons*, 1993. 29 x 24 x 5. Collection of Dr. and Mrs. Richard Basch (SA1293.03.07).

Pages 78 and 79 (detail)
*Suspended Artifact: Buffalo Pouch with Orinka*, 1995. 36 x 32 x 6. Private collection (SA195.01.06).

Page 80
*Suspended Artifact: Pouch with Tusks*, 1993. 27 x 25 x 5.
Collection of Dale and Doug Anderson (SA593.06.08).

Page 81
*Suspended Artifact: Gourd with Rhino Horns*, 1995.
27 x 25 x 9. Private collection (SA595.24.09).

Page 82, left
Detail, *Suspended Artifact*, 1995 (see pages 102–3).

Page 82, right
*Suspended Artifact: Antler and Tusks*, 1994. 36 x 19 x 15.
Private collection (SA594.09.06).

Page 83
*Suspended Artifact: Quiver with Orinkas*, 1993. 30 x 22 x 5.
Collection of Francine and Benson Pilloff (SA593.17.08).

Page 84
*Canopic Jar: Mountain Goat*, 1992. 33 x 13. Collection of
Serge Lechaczynski, Galerie Internationale du Verre,
Biot, France (CJ1192.07.02).

Page 85, top left
*Canopic Jar: Panther*, 1992. 31 x 11. Collection of Sylvia
and Eric Elsesser (CJ1192.03.02).

Page 85, top right
*Canopic Jar: Hawk*, 1992. 26 x 12. Collection of Nancy
and Philip Kotler (CJ1292.01.02).

Page 85, bottom left
*Canopic Jar: Sable Antelope*, 1995. 48 x 11. Collection of
Beth and Anthony Terrana (CJ595.01.02).

Page 85, bottom right
*Canopic Jar: African Bull*, 1995. 47 x 17. Collection of
Sylvia and Eric Elsesser (CJ195.01.02).

Page 86, top
Detail, *Artifact Bundles: Ravens*, 1995. Private collection
(A595.04.02, A595.05.02).

Page 86, bottom
*Suspended Artifact: Mask with Quiver*, 1995. 32 x 24 x 10.
Collection of Gerard L. Cafesjian (SA395.01.10).

Page 87
*Suspended Artifact: Raven Bundle and Lashed Antler*,
1995. 34 x 21 x 12. Collection of Barbara and Ron Balser
(SA595.07.06).

Pages 88–89
Grouping, *Artifact: Tooth*, 1994. Limited edition series
commissioned by Seattle Art Museum.

Page 90
*Artifact: Tooth*, 1995. 15 x 22 x 13. Collection of Mr. and
Mrs. Lars Wetterling (AT595.01.02).

Page 91
*Artifact: Tooth*, 1993. 15 x 23 x 12. Collection of Bruce R.
McCaw (AT593.01.02).

Pages 92–93
*Artifact: Tooth*, 1993. 12 x 18 x 13. Private collection
(AT593.02.02).

Pages 94 and 95 (detail)
*Suspended Artifact: Pouch with Lashed Scoop*, 1995.
27 x 24 x 5. Collection of the artist (SA595.02.07).

Page 96
*Suspended Artifact: Scoop with Legged Pouch*, 1995.
27 x 21 x 5. Private collection (SA595.01.06).

Page 97
*Suspended Artifact: Baleen and Walrus Tusk*, 1995.
41 x 29 x 10. Private collection (SA595.13.07).

Pages 98 (detail) and 99
*Suspended Artifact: Horn Scoops with Lashed Antler*, 1995.
29 x 21 x 8. Private collection (SA595.12.06).

Page 100
*Suspended Artifact: Pouch with Tusk and Bone Pins*, 1994.
30 x 30 x 9. Private collection (SA1094.05.12).

Page 101, top
*Suspended Artifact: Pouch with Tusk*, 1994. 30 x 26 x 6.
Collection of The St. Paul Companies, Minn.
(SA1094.02.06).

Page 101, bottom
*Suspended Artifact: Pouch with Orinka*, 1993. 29 x 25 x 9.
Collection of Mr. and Mrs. A. Huda Farouki
(SA1293.06.13).

Page 102
*Suspended Artifact: Pouch with Baton*, 1995. 36 x 20 x 7.
Private collection (SA395.08.08).

Pages 102–3
*Suspended Artifact: Walrus Tusk with Lashed Antler*, 1995.
24 x 27 x 10. Private collection (SA395.07.06).

Pages 104 and 105 (detail)
*Suspended Artifact: Antlered Spoon with Scoop and Gourd*,
1995. 28 x 23 x 6. Private collection (SA595.05.07).

Page 106
*Suspended Artifact: Scoop with Lashed Antler and Tusks*,
1995. 31 x 20 x 6. Private collection (SA595.11.06).

Page 107
*Suspended Artifact: Raven Mask with Antlered Spoon and
Rhino Horn*, 1995. 29 x 23 x 8. Collection of the artist
(SA595.26.07).

Page 128
*Canopic Jar: Defassa Water Buck*, 1994. 48 x 13. Collection
of Ronald and Susan Crowell (CJ394.01.02).

# BIOGRAPHY

Born July 25, 1957, Carmel, California

## EDUCATION

California State University, Chico
Central Washington University, Ellensburg

## RECENT SOLO EXHIBITIONS

1996  Susan Duval Gallery, Aspen, Colo.
Friesen Gallery, Sun Valley, Idaho
IMAGO Gallery, Palm Desert, Calif.
Kennesaw State College Gallery of Art,
    Marietta, Ga.
Meadows Museum of Art, Centenary College,
    Shreveport, La.

1995  Everett Center for the Arts, Everett, Wash.
Foster/White Gallery, Kirkland and Seattle, Wash.
Habatat Galleries, Boca Raton, Fla.
Maurine Littleton Gallery, Washington, D.C.
Riley Hawk Galleries, Cleveland and Columbus,
    Ohio
Lisa Sette Gallery, Scottsdale, Ariz.

1994  Susan Duval Gallery, Aspen, Colo.
Friesen Gallery, Sun Valley, Idaho
Habatat Galleries, Farmington Hills, Mich.
Dorothy Weiss Gallery, San Francisco

1993  Habatat Galleries, Boca Raton, Fla.
Heller Gallery, New York
Maurine Littleton Gallery, Washington, D.C.
Betsy Rosenfield Gallery, Chicago
Laura Russo Gallery, Portland, Ore.

1992  Foster/White Gallery, Seattle
Friesen Gallery, Sun Valley, Idaho
Lisa Sette Gallery, Scottsdale, Ariz.

1991  Charles Grant Gallery, Ketchum, Idaho
Helander Gallery, Palm Beach, Fla.
Maurine Littleton Gallery, Washington, D.C.
Riley Hawk Galleries, Cleveland and Columbus

1990  Foster/White Gallery, Seattle
Maurine Littleton Gallery, Washington, D.C.
Betsy Rosenfield Gallery, Chicago

1989  Riley Hawk Galleries, Cleveland and Columbus
Brendan Walter Gallery, Santa Monica, Calif.

1988  Foster/White Gallery, Seattle
Glass Art Gallery of Toronto, Canada

Maurine Littleton Gallery, Washington, D.C.
Skagit Valley College, Mt. Vernon, Wash.
University of Michigan, Dearborn
Brendan Walter Gallery, Santa Monica, Calif.

1987  Heller Gallery, New York
Holsten Galleries, Palm Beach, Fla.

## SELECTED GROUP EXHIBITIONS

1996  *American Glass: Masters of the Art,* United States
    Information Agency (international traveling
    exhibition)

1995  *American Art Glass,* Halls Gallery, Hallmark
    Headquarters, Kansas City, Mo.
*Breaking Barriers: Recent American Craft,* Portland
    Art Museum, Portland, Ore.
*Contemporary Northwest Art,* Coos Art Museum,
    Coos Bay, Ore.
*Glass America,* Heller Gallery, New York
*Glass as Art,* Blue Spiral 1, Asheville, N.C.
*Glass Now, World Studio Glass Exhibition,* Yamaha
    Corporation, Tokyo
*International Survey of Contemporary Art Glass,*
    Wood Street Gallery and Concept Art Gallery,
    Pittsburgh
*Northwest Glass: Part I,* Museum of Northwest
    Art, LaConner, Wash.
*Sculpture,* Galerie Internationale du Verre, Biot,
    France
*Taipei International Glass Exhibition,* Taiwan
*A Touch of Glass,* Explorers Hall, National Geo-
    graphic Society, Washington, D.C.

1994  *Birds and Beasts,* Seattle Art Museum
*Breaking Barriers: Recent American Craft,*
    American Craft Museum, New York
*Collective Brilliance,* Albany Museum of Art, Ga.
*Form and Light: Contemporary Glass from
    the Permanent Collection,* American Craft
    Museum, New York
*Glass Masters,* Helander Gallery, Palm Beach, Fla.
*Masterworks of Contemporary Glass,* Habatat
    Galleries, Farmington Hills, Mich.
*Pilchuck Glass at the Monte Cristo,* Everett Center
    for the Arts, Everett, Wash.
*World Glass Now, '94,* Hokkaidō Museum of
    Modern Art, Sapporo, Japan

1993  *Formed by Fire,* Carnegie Museum of Art,
    Pittsburgh
*Glass Installations,* American Craft Museum,
    New York
*Maximizing the Minimum,* Museum of American
    Glass, Millville, N.J.

*SOFA,* represented by Betsy Rosenfield Gallery, Chicago

*21st Annual International Invitational,* Habatat Galleries, Farmington Hills, Mich.

*Verriales '93,* Galerie Internationale du Verre, Biot, France

*Where Image Meets Form,* Habatat Galleries, Boca Raton, Fla.

1992 *Clearly Art: The Pilchuck Legacy,* Whatcom Museum of History and Art, Bellingham, Wash. (touring through 1995)

*First International Exhibition of Contemporary Glass in Latin America,* Rufino Tamayo Museum, Mexico City, and the Marco, Monterrey, Mexico

*International Exhibition of Glass Kanazawa '92,* Kanazawa, Japan

1991 *Artists at Work,* Cheney Cowles Museum, Spokane, Wash., and Boise Art Museum, Idaho

*Contemporary Glass: Seven Northwest Artists,* Laura Russo Gallery, Portland, Ore.

*Focus Northwest,* Old Pueblo Museum, Tucson

*Frozen Moments: Glass Artists of the Northwest,* Bellevue Art Museum, Wash.

*Masters of Contemporary Glass,* Philharmonic Center for the Arts Galleries, Naples, Fla.

*Out of the Fire,* William Traver Gallery, Seattle

*Studio Glass: Selections from the David Jacob Chodorkoff Collection,* The Detroit Institute of Arts

1990 *Glassworks,* Renwick Gallery, Smithsonian Institution, Washington, D.C.

Nielsen Gallery, Stockholm Art Fair, Sweden

1989 *Artful Objects: Recent American Craft,* Fort Wayne Museum of Art

*Documents Northwest: Figures of Translucence,* Seattle Art Museum

1988 *A Generation in Glass Sculpture,* Florida State University, Tallahassee

*Craft Today: Poetry of the Physical,* traveling exhibition: American Craft Museum, New York; The Denver Art Museum, Colo.; Laguna Art Museum, Laguna Beach, Calif.; Milwaukee Art Museum; J. B. Speed Art Museum, Louisville; Virginia Museum of Fine Arts, Richmond; San Diego Art Museum

*Pilchuck School: The Great Northwest Glass Experiment,* Bellevue Art Museum, Wash.

1987 *Contemporary Glass,* Abilene Fine Arts Museum, Abilene, Tex.

*New Expressions with Glass,* Hunter Museum of Art, Chattanooga, Tenn.

*Thirty Years of New Glass, 1957–1987,* The Corning Museum of Glass, Corning, N.Y., and the Toledo Museum of Art

## TEACHING EXPERIENCE AND LECTURES

1979–present

Pilchuck Glass School, Stanwood, Wash.

1995 Artist's Lecture, Memphis Brooks Museum of Art, Memphis

1994 *The Art of Glass,* seminar, The Bon Marché, Seattle

Niijima Art Glass Center, Tokyo

1993 Creative Glass Center of America, demonstrating artist at Glassweekend '93, Wheaton Village, Millville, N.J.

1992 California College of Arts and Crafts, Oakland

Niijima Art Glass Center, Tokyo

1991 University of Hawaii at Manoa

1988 Penland School of Crafts, N.C.

1987 Appalachian Center for Crafts, Smithville, Tenn.

1986 Canadian Glass Art Society Symposium, Toronto

New Zealand Society of Artists in Glass, Aukland

1985 Art Glass Academy, Vienna

Haystack Mountain School of Crafts, Deer Isle, Me.

New York Experimental Glass Workshop

## RECENT AWARDS

1994 National Endowment for the Arts, Individual Artist Grant

## SELECTED BIBLIOGRAPHY

Susan Biskborn. *Artists at Work: 25 Northwest Glassmakers, Ceramists and Jewelers.* Seattle: Alaska Northwest Books, 1991.

Gary Blonston. "Through a Glass Artfully." *Art and Antiques,* Dec. 1993, pp. 58–63.

*Collective Brilliance: Contemporary Glass.* Exh. cat. Albany, Ga.: Albany Museum of Art, 1994.

*Contemporary Glass.* Exh. cat. Fort Lauderdale, Fla.: Museum of Art, 1993.

Holland Cotter. "Glass Sculptors Whose Work Transcends Craft." *New York Times,* June 18, 1993.

Roger Downey. "Sacred Bone Yard." *Seattle Weekly,* Oct. 21, 1992.

Mary Daniels. "Glass Artifacts: An Artist's Works Reflect Archeology." *Chicago Tribune,* Sep. 2, 1990.

Kate Elliott, ed. *William Morris: Artifact and Art.* Seattle: University of Washington Press, 1989.

Patricia Failing. "William Morris Glass Remains." *American Craft,* Feb./Mar. 1993, pp. 49–51.

Matthew Kangas. "Glass Art." *Artnews,* Jan. 1995, pp. 49–78.

———. "Paleoglass." *Glass,* spring 1994, pp. 20–29.

Morton A. Kaplan. "Primal Instincts." *The World and I,* Jan. 1993, pp. 212–21.

Donna Loyle. "Ageless Imagery in a Modern World." *American Style,* vol. 1, no. 1 (winter 1995), pp. 28–30.

Bonnie Miller. *Out of the Fire: Northwest Artists and Their Work.* San Francisco: Chronicle Books, 1991.

Sylvia Netzer. "William Morris." *New Glass,* March 1993, pp. 12–21.

Todd Powell. "Collective Works." *Horizon Air,* Aug. 1994, pp. 20–25.

Satoka Shinoda. "William Morris." *Glass and Art,* no. 8 (1995), pp. 42–51.

Robin Updike. "Glass Explorer." *Seattle Times,* Jan. 24, 1995.

*World Glass Now '94.* Exh. cat. Sapporo, Japan: Hokkaidō Museum of Modern Art, 1994.

# SELECTED PUBLIC COLLECTIONS

American Craft Museum, New York

Auckland Museum, New Zealand

Birmingham Museum of Art

The Carnegie Museum of Art, Pittsburgh

The Corning Museum of Glass, Corning, N.Y.

Davis Wright Tremaine, Seattle

Delta Airlines, Portland, Oregon

Edmonds Arts Commission, Wash.

First Union Bank, Charlotte, N.C.

Florida National Collection, Florida National Bank, Jacksonville

Hokkaidō Museum of Modern Art, Sapporo, Japan

Hunter Museum of Art, Chattanooga

IBM Corporation, Tulsa

J. B. Speed Art Museum, Louisville

Joslyn Art Museum, Omaha

Los Angeles County Museum of Art, Los Angeles

McDonald's Corporation, Oakbrook, Ill., and Bellevue, Wash.

The Metropolitan Museum of Art, New York

Microsoft Corporation, Redmond, Wash.

Missoula Museum of the Arts

The Mobile Museum of Art

Musée des Arts Décoratifs, Paris

Museum für Kunst und Gewerbe, Hamburg

Museum of American Glass, Millville, N.J.

Museum of Art, Rhode Island School of Design, Providence

Pilchuck Collection, Stanwood, Wash.

The Pilchuck Glass Collection at City Centre and U.S. Bank Center, Seattle

Port of Seattle

Rockefeller Center, New York

Royal College of Art, London

Safeco Insurance Company, Seattle

Seattle Art Museum

Seattle-First National Bank Collection, Seattle

Seattle Repertory Theatre

Seattle-Tacoma International Airport, Permanent Installation

Security Pacific Collection, Security Pacific Bank, Seattle

Sheldon Memorial Art Gallery and Sculpture Garden, University of Nebraska-Lincoln

Sheraton Seattle Hotel and Towers Collection

Shimonoseki City Art Museum, Japan

State Foundation of Culture in the Arts, Honolulu

State of Oregon Public Services Building, Portland

The Toledo Museum of Art

Toyota USA Corporate Retreat, Hilo, Hawaii

UPS Corporate Collection, Louisville

United Airlines, San Francisco

University of Michigan, Dearborn

U.S. News & World Report, Washington, D.C.

The Valley National Bank of Arizona, Tucson

Victoria and Albert Museum, London

Virginia Museum of Fine Arts, Richmond

Westin Hotel, San Francisco

# ACKNOWLEDGMENTS

I would like to acknowledge the people that made this work possible: Jon Ormbrek for twenty years of friendship and dedication; the glassblowing team, Randy Walker and Karen Willenbrink, for their tireless effort; and special thanks to Holle Simmons for facilitating this project and affording me the opportunity to focus on the work.

I would also like to express my deepest gratitude to the three great artists who have inspired me: Dale Chihuly, Judy Pfaff, and Italo Scanga. Additional thanks to Pilchuck Glass School for allowing me to work in such a great facility.

**William Morris**

| DATE DUE | |
|---|---|
| MAR 1 5 2002 | |
| | |
| | |
| | |
| | |
| | |
| | |
| | |
| | |
| | |
| | |
| | |
| | |
| | |
| | |